Understanding and Analyzing
FINANCIAL
STATEMENTS
A Project-Based Approach

Fourth Edition

KAREN P. SCHOENEBECK

PEARSON

Prentice
Hall

Upper Saddle River, New Jersey 07458

Library of Congress Cataloging-in-Publication Data
Schoenebeck, Karen P.
  Understanding and analyzing financial statements : a project based approach / Karen P.
Schoenebeck. — 4th ed.
    p. cm.
  Previously published under title: Interpreting and analyzing financial statements.
  ISBN 0-13-239190-2 (alk. paper)
  1. Financial statements—Case studies. 2. Asset-liability management—Case studies. 3.
Corporations—Investments—Case studies. 4. Ratio analysis. I. Schoenebeck, Karen P.
Interpreting and analyzing financial statements. II. Title.

  HG4028.B2S39 2007

2006049640

AVP/Executive Editor: Steve Sartori
VP/Editorial Director: Jeff Shelstad
Editorial Project Manager: Kerri Tomasso
Managing Editor (Production): Cynthia Zonneveld
Production Editor: Melissa Feimer
Permissions Supervisor: Charles Morris
Manufacturing Buyer: Michelle Klein
Cover Photo: Images.com

Credits and acknowledgments borrowed from other sources and reproduced, with permission, in this textbook
appear on appropriate page within text.

Pearson Education LTD.
Pearson Education Singapore, Pte. Ltd
Pearson Education, Canada, Ltd
Pearson Education–Japan

Pearson Education Australia PTY, Limited
Pearson Education North Asia Ltd
Pearson Educación de Mexico, S.A. de C.V.
Pearson Education Malaysia, Pte. Ltd

1 0 9 8 7 6 5
ISBN 0-13-239190-2

TABLE OF CONTENTS

CHAPTER 4: STATEMENT OF CASH FLOWS

PREFACE

This book uses the financial statement analysis approach to introduce accounting and can be used to supplement any financial accounting text. All of the activities have been classroom tested over the past ten years and enthusiastically received at both the undergraduate and graduate level.

WHY THESE ACTIVITIES WERE DEVELOPED

When I first started assigning a comprehensive financial statement analysis as a capstone project, it became evident many students didn't know where to begin. They were overwhelmed by all of the numbers and felt frustrated. As a result, this series of preliminary activities was developed to prepare students for the capstone project. Each activity concentrates on only one aspect of financial statement analysis. After completing the preliminary activities, students feel confident in their strategies and ability to successfully complete a comprehensive financial statement analysis.

USING DATA FROM WELL-KNOWN CORPORATIONS

These activities use financial data from companies familiar to students. The actual numbers make the class relevant and more interesting to students. Because students are already familiar with the companies, they more easily grasp the material and remember the concepts.

FOCUS IS ON INTERPRETING AND ANALYZING

Most amounts are provided and calculations are kept to a minimum so students can focus their time and attention on interpretation and analysis.

RATIO ANALYSIS

Activities point out the significant role ratios have in analyzing financial statements. Students acquire a "feel" for the expected range and magnitude of the ratios and identify whether a high or low ratio is usually preferred. Commonly used ratios are studied.

TREND PERCENTAGES AND COMMON-SIZE STATEMENT ANALYSIS

Emphasis is placed on comparing the rate of increase or decrease of various account classifications within each financial statement. Common-size statements are used to compare companies of different size.

FOUR-YEAR COMPARISON

Financial statements are introduced using four years of comparative information. Each line item is studied and the student develops an overall strategy to analyze the financial statement. Questions lead to increased understanding and highlight important trends.

ETHICAL ISSUES

Ethical issues are incorporated into a number of the activities.

RANGE AND MAGNITUDE OF AMOUNTS

Companies are carefully selected so students get a "feel" for the range and magnitude of expected amounts and ratios in the corporate world.

REVIEW

Review exercises titled "Test Your Understanding" are located at the end of most chapters. In addition, Chapter 5 provides a thorough review of individual balance sheet accounts and Chapter 6 provides a comprehensive review of all the financial statements.

CLASS FORMAT

These activities can be utilized as individual homework assignments, small-group discussions in class, a review, or a combination of all three. Whichever approach is used, these assignments result in greater understanding and lively classroom discussion.

CORPORATE RESEARCH AND ANALYSIS

The final project requires students to research, analyze, and prepare a comprehensive written report and presentation on the public corporation of their choice. To complete the project, students must obtain a copy of the corporate financial statements and utilize a variety of resources. Because the company is the student's choice, interest is high and a quality product results. This project has several parts. The parts may be assigned throughout the semester or as a capstone project at the end.

TO THE INSTRUCTOR...

This book contains a series of activities designed to help students acquire the necessary skills to interpret, analyze, and research financial statement information. A user-oriented approach is maintained throughout the book, utilizing financial information from companies familiar to students. For successful completion of the problem materials, both a conceptual understanding and mathematical computations are required. Activities employ written exercises, Internet activities, and other research opportunities to strengthen understanding. Ethical issues are raised. With over 50 activities to choose from, instructors can select activities appropriate to their needs.

Chapter 1 is designed to accompany the first few weeks of a semester course. Basic accounting concepts are reinforced. An early introduction of ratios, trend analysis, and common-size statements enhance understanding of the relationship between amounts on the balance sheet and the income statement throughout the course. The analysis activities require no previous introduction.

Chapters 2, 3, and 4 are designed as a step-by-step guide for analyzing each of the three major financial statements. Questions lead to increased understanding and highlight important trends. These activities can be assigned anytime after the first few weeks of a semester course. They can be used concurrently with the financial statement coverage in the text, after the statement coverage as a review to reinforce understanding, or simply as a stand-alone assignment at any point throughout the semester. The activities in these chapters start basic and progress to more complex.

Chapter 5 should be used throughout the semester as the topics arise. Specific balance sheet account information is presented followed by a series of questions that test for understanding. A thorough understanding of the material is required for successful completion. The later activities examine the stock and bond markets, which enhance the coverage of liabilities and stockholders' equity.

Chapter 6 provides a comprehensive review of all three major financial statements. The activities review understanding of transaction analysis, finding specific account information, interpreting financial information, and analyzing all three major financial statements.

Chapter 7 is a Corporate Analysis project with six parts. It can be assigned as a capstone project at the end of the semester or as a series of assignments spread throughout the semester. This final project requires students to research, analyze, and prepare a comprehensive, written report and presentation on the public corporation of their choice. This project provides an opportunity to apply and reinforce learning from all previous activities and from the accounting course.

Have fun with these assignments. Bring real-world numbers into the classroom in an organized series of assignments. My students enjoy these assignments and the learning that results. I hope you do too. Please feel free to contact me with comments and questions regarding these activities. My e-mail address is karen@twopavedroads.com

Karen Schoenebeck, author

TO THE STUDENT...

WARNING!!!
MANY OF THE QUESTIONS CONTAINED IN THIS BOOK REQUIRE THOUGHT!

You are about to embark on a journey into the world of business. Some of you read *The Wall Street Journal* on a regular basis, while others have not yet been introduced to assets and liabilities. This series of activities is designed to introduce you to the financial information of a variety of familiar companies and financial statement analysis. After completing these activities you should feel confident in your ability to research and understand any set of corporate financial statements. Below is a summary of each chapter followed by a question answered in the chapter material.

Chapter 1 introduces the range and magnitude of amounts reported on financial statements of well-known companies. Ratios, trend indexes, and common-size statements are introduced. *For major corporations, are sales usually reported in the range of millions, billions, or trillions?*

Chapters 2, 3, and 4 introduce strategies for analyzing the financial statements and then applying those strategies. Trend indexes and common-size statements are prepared followed by questions that lead to interpretation and understanding.

Chapter 2: *Does an increase in retained earnings indicate the company issued more stock, purchased more assets, or reported net income?*

Chapter 3: *If sales increase by 10% would you also expect expenses to increase?*

Chapter 4: *The primary source of cash for an established company with a strong cash position should be operating, investing, or financing activities?*

Chapter 5 reinforces understanding amounts reported on the financial statements. It also examines the stock and bond market and benchmarks current interest rates and the Dow Jones Industrial Average. *For property, plant, and equipment (PPE), is acquisition cost or book value added to calculate total assets?*

Chapter 6 provides a comprehensive review of all three major financial statements. The activities review understanding of transaction analysis, understanding specific account information, interpreting financial information, and analyzing all three major financial statements. *When using LIFO, the most recent (current) inventory costs are reported on which financial statement?*

Chapter 7 is a comprehensive project that requires researching and analyzing a publicly traded corporation of your choice.

ABOUT THE AUTHOR

KAREN SCHOENEBECK, C.P.A., received her M.B.A. from the University of Minnesota.

EMPLOYMENT HISTORY
- **Professor of Accounting** with more than twenty years of teaching experience at University of California – Santa Barbara; Wichita State University, Kansas; St. Norbert College, Wisconsin; and Southwestern College, Kansas at both the undergraduate and graduate levels.
- **Public accounting experience** with BKD (Baird, Kurtz, and Dobson) in Kansas; Shinners, Hucovski, and Company, S.C. (now Schenck Business Solutions) in Wisconsin; and most recently Jones, Wheeler, and Company in California.
- **Administrative experience** as MBA Program Director at Southwestern College, Kansas.

PUBLISHED AUTHOR of accounting books and supplementary materials including:
- Karen Schoenebeck, *Test Item File*, to accompany *Cost Accounting: A Managerial Emphasis*, eleventh edition, by Horngren, Datar, and Foster published by Prentice Hall, 2003. (833 pages)
- Karen Schoenebeck, *Test Item File*, to accompany *Management Accounting*, fourth edition, by Atkinson, Kaplan, and Young published by Prentice Hall, 2004. (450 pages)

LEADERSHIP TRAINING PRACTITIONER presenting at national conferences on topics that include, but are not limited to: *Collaborative Skills: Building Effective Teams, Negotiating Conflict Situations, Essential Skills for Managing Change, Resolving Ethical Issues, Facilitation Skills, and Goal Setting and Career Planning.*

SERVICE TO PROFESSIONAL ORGANIZATIONS includes over ten years of service on national board of directors of various accounting organizations and for the 1999-2000 term as National President of the Educational Foundation for Women in Accounting.

TRAVEL AND THE ARTS...an avid interest and so leads travel tours to Europe and Southeast Asia and promotes traveling independently overseas.

ACKNOWLEDGMENTS

I WOULD LIKE TO THANK...

The Prentice Hall staff including Deborah Hoffman who discovered my materials and encouraged me to submit them for publishing.

My students who provide continued opportunities for me to learn and are always ready to give me honest and helpful feedback.

My friends who continue to support my writing and encourage me to try various other endeavors.

Karen Schoenebeck, author

CHAPTER 1 – INTRODUCTION

Activity 1   **THE FOUR FINANCIAL STATEMENTS**

Purpose: ·   Identify the four financial statements
              ·   Understand the basic information provided by each financial statement

```
            BALANCE SHEET
    Assets    | Liabilities
              | Stockholders'
              |    equity
```

The Balance Sheet (B/S) provides a snapshot of a company's financial position as of a certain date. It reports **assets,** items of value such as inventory and equipment, and whether the assets are financed with **liabilities** (debt) or **stockholders' equity** (equity).

```
         INCOME STATEMENT
            Revenues
           (Expenses)
           Net income
```

The Income Statement (I/S) reports the company's profitability during an accounting period. It reports **revenues,** amounts received from customers for products sold or services provided, and **expenses,** the costs incurred to produce revenues. The difference is **net income.**

```
    STATEMENT OF RETAINED EARNINGS
       Retained earnings, beginning
            + Net income
             (Dividends)
       Retained earnings, ending
```

The Statement of Retained Earnings (R/E) reports if the **earnings** (net income) of this accounting period are distributed as **dividends** or retained in the business as **retained earnings**.

```
      STATEMENT OF CASH FLOWS
           Cash inflows
          (Cash outflows)
       Change in the cash account
```

The Statement of Cash Flows (C/F) reports cash inflows and cash outflows during an accounting period.

Q1   Which financial statement reports…
     a.   dividends declared by the board of directors for shareholders? (**BS / IS / RE / CF**)
     b.   the amount of cash received from customers during the accounting period? (**BS / IS / RE / CF**)
     c.   whether the company was profitable or not? (**BS / IS / RE / CF**)
     d.   whether assets are primarily financed with debt or equity? (**BS / IS / RE / CF**)
     e.   the revenues of a corporation? (**BS / IS / RE / CF**)
     f.   the liabilities of a corporation? (**BS / IS / RE / CF**)
     g.   the balance of retained earnings at the beginning of the accounting period? (**BS / IS / RE / CF**)
     h.   the information as of a certain date? (**BS / IS / RE / CF**)
     i.   the information over a period of time? (**BS / IS / RE / CF**)

BALANCE SHEET (B/S)

Purpose:
· Understand the information provided by the balance sheet
· Identify asset, liability, and stockholders equity accounts reported on the balance sheet
· Understand the accounting equation

PEPSICO (PEP*) 12/31/2005 BALANCE SHEET ($ in millions)				
ASSETS		**LIABILITIES**		
Cash and cash equivalents	$ 1,716	Accounts payable		$ 5,971
Short-term investments	3,166	Short-term debt		2,889
Accounts receivable, net	3,261	Other current liabilities		546
Inventories	1,693	Long-term debt		2,313
Other current assets	618	Other non-current liabilities		5,688
Property, plant, and equipment, net	8,681			
Goodwill	4,088	**STOCKHOLDERS' EQUITY**		
Other intangibles	1,616	Contributed capital		644
Long-term investments	3,485	Retained earnings		21,116
Other non-current assets	3,403	Other stockholders' equity		(7,440)
TOTAL ASSETS	$31,727	**TOTAL L & SE**		$31,727

The balance sheet reports assets and the amount of assets financed with liabilities and stockholders' equity as of a certain date. The accounting equation is: **Assets = Liabilities + Stockholders' Equity**

Assets are all items of value that a corporation has a right to use. Typical asset accounts include cash, accounts receivable, inventory, equipment, buildings, and land. Accounts *receivable* are amounts to be *received* in the future by the corporation from customers.

Liabilities are amounts owed to creditors; the amount of debt owed to third parties. Typical liability accounts include accounts payable, wages payable, notes payable, and bonds payable. The key word found in many liability accounts is *payable*. Accounts *payable* are amounts to be *paid* in the future by the corporation to suppliers.

Stockholders' Equity is the portion of assets the owners own free and clear. Stockholders' equity may also be referred to as shareholders' equity or owners' equity.
    Typical stockholders' equity accounts include:
    Contributed Capital -- amounts paid (contributed) by stockholders to purchase common stock and
        preferred stock.
    Retained Earnings -- net income earned by the company since its incorporation and not yet distributed as
        dividends.

Q1   Assets can either be financed with _____ or _____.

Q2   Identify the accounting equation amounts for PepsiCo Corporation using the information above.

    Assets $_____ million =
    Liabilities $_____ million + Stockholders' Equity $_____ million

Q3   Will the accounting equation hold true for every corporation? (**Yes / No / Can't tell**)   Why?

* Stock market symbols are shown in parentheses.

Q4   Circle whether the account is classified as an (A)sset, (L)iability, or part of stockholders' equity (SE) on the balance sheet.

    a.   Cash   (A / L / SE)

    b.   Retained earnings   (A / L / SE)

    c.   Notes payable   (A / L / SE)

    d.   Accounts receivable   (A / L / SE)

    e.   Equipment   (A / L / SE)

    f.   Mortgage payable   (A / L / SE)

    g.   Common stock   (A / L / SE)

    h.   Building   (A / L / SE)

    i.   Inventory   (A / L / SE)

    j.   Bonds payable   (A / L / SE)

    k.   Land   (A / L / SE)

Q5   Use PepsiCo's balance sheet on the previous page to answer the following questions:

    a.   What amount does this company expect to receive from customers within the next few months?
        $_____ million

    b.   The title of the largest asset account is _____ reporting $_____ million.

        The costs of what types of assets would be included in this account?

    c.   How much does this company currently owe suppliers? $_____ million

    d.   Since the company started business, what is the total amount shareholders have paid for their shares of stock? $_____ million

    e.   Since the company started business, how much net income was earned and not yet distributed as dividends? $_____ million

INCOME STATEMENT (I/S)

Purpose:
- Understand the information reported on the income statement
- Identify revenue and expense accounts reported on the income statement

PEPSICO (PEP) 2005 INCOME STATEMENT ($ in millions)	
Sales revenue	$32,562
Cost of goods sold	13,018
Gross profit	19,544
Selling, general, and administrative expense	12,314
Depreciation and amortization expense	1,308
Other revenues and expenses	460
Income before income tax	6,382
Provision for income tax	2,304
Net income	$ 4,078

The income statement reports the company's profitability during an accounting period.

Revenues are gross amounts received from customers for products sold and services provided. *Sales revenue* and *service revenue* are amounts earned engaging in the primary business activity.

Expenses are the costs incurred to produce revenues. Expenses are recorded in the accounting period they benefit (if a cause and effect relationship exists) or are incurred (if there is no cause and effect relationship). *Cost of goods sold* expense reports the wholesale costs of inventory sold during the accounting period.

Net income is revenues less expenses. Net income is also referred to as *profit (loss)*, *earnings*, or the *bottom line*.

Revenues – Expenses = Net income

Q1 Circle whether the account is classified as a (R)evenue, (E)xpense, or (Not) reported on the income statement.

a.	Wage expense	**(R / E / Not)**	d.	Cash	**(R / E / Not)**
b.	Inventory	**(R / E / Not)**	e.	Building	**(R / E / Not)**
c.	Cost of goods sold	**(R / E / Not)**	f.	Service revenue	**(R / E / Not)**

Q2 Review PepsiCo's 2005 income statement above and answer the following questions:

a. This company reports (**1 / 3 / 4 / 5**) revenue accounts and (**1 / 3 / 4 / 5**) expense accounts.

b. What amount of beverages and snacks were sold to customers? $_____ million

c. The title of the largest expense account is _____ reporting $_____ million, which is typically the largest expense account for a company within the (**retail / service**) industry. What specific types of costs would be included in this account for PepsiCo?

d. Was PepsiCo profitable?   (**Yes / No**)   How much profit was reported? $_____ million

Q3 Net income can also be referred to as (**revenues / expenses / common stock / earnings**).

STATEMENT OF RETAINED EARNINGS (R/E)

Purpose:
- · Understand information provided by the Statement of Retained Earnings
- · Identify relationships between the IS, RE, and the BS
- · Understand information provided by the Statement of Cash Flows

PEPSICO (PEP) 2005 STATEMENT OF RETAINED EARNINGS ($ in millions)	
Retained earnings, beginning	$18,730
+ Net income (earnings of this accounting period)	4,078
- Dividends (earnings distributed to shareholders)	(1,692)
= Retained earnings, ending	$21,116

The statement of retained earnings reports changes within the retained earnings account during an accounting period. Retained earnings is increased by **net income** (earnings) of the accounting period and decreased when earnings are distributed as **dividends** to the stockholders. Earnings that are not distributed as dividends are reported as retained earnings.

Q1   Earnings is another word for (**revenue / receivables / net income**).
Earnings of a corporation belong to the (**managers / stockholders**).
Earnings can either be distributed to the stockholders as (**dividends / interest / expenses / retained earnings**) or kept in the business as (**dividends / interest / expenses / retained earnings**).

Q2   Income statement: Revenues - Expenses = _____
Statement of R/E: Beg R/E + _____ - Dividends = _____
Stockholders' equity = Contributed capital + _____
Balance sheet: Assets = _____ + _____

Q3   Net income is computed on the (**IS / RE / BS**) and then transferred to the Statement of Retained Earnings. Retained Earnings at the end of the accounting period is computed on the Statement of Retained Earnings and then transferred to the (**IS / RE / BS**).

Q4   Circle whether the account/information is reported on the Income Statement (IS), Statement of Retained Earnings (RE), or the Balance Sheet (BS). Note: *Some amounts are reported on two statements.*

a. Wage expense	(**IS/RE/BS**)	f. Sales revenue	(**IS/RE/BS**)
b. Bonds payable	(**IS/RE/BS**)	g. Dividends	(**IS/RE/BS**)
c. Cost of goods sold	(**IS/RE/BS**)	h. Buildings	(**IS/RE/BS**)
d. Common stock	(**IS/RE/BS**)	i. Net income	(**IS/RE/BS**)
e. Accounts receivable	(**IS/RE/BS**)	j. Retained earnings	(**IS/RE/BS**)

STATEMENT OF CASH FLOWS (C/F)

PEPSICO (PEP) 2005 STATEMENT OF CASH FLOWS ($ in millions)	
Net cash from operating activities (NCOA)	$5,852
Net cash from investing activities (NCIA)	(3,517)
Net cash from financing activities (NCFA)	(1,878)
Effect of exchange rate changes	(21)
Change in cash	436
+ Cash, beginning of the period	1,280
= Cash, end of the period	$1,716

Q5   For the above statement, the amount reported for cash at the end of the accounting period is also reported on the (**Balance Sheet / Income Statement / Statement of Retained Earnings**).

Activity 5 **GENERALLY ACCEPTED ACCOUNTING PRINCIPLES (GAAP)**

Purpose: · Understand that GAAP (Generally Accepted Accounting Principles) are the rules of financial accounting
· Apply the historical cost principle

GAAP (Generally Accepted Accounting Principles) are the rules that must be followed by management when preparing financial statements that are available to investors.

- The **SEC** (Securities and Exchange Commission) has legislative authority to set the reporting rules for accounting information of the publicly-held corporations it regulates. It has designated GAAP to be the official rules. The SEC provides oversight and enforcement authority over the Financial Accounting Standards Board (FASB) and the Public Company Accounting Oversight Board (PCAOB).

- Currently, the seven full-time voting members of the **FASB** (Financial Accounting Standards Board) help to set accounting reporting standards and formulate GAAP.

- **Audits** attest to whether a company's financial statements comply with GAAP. Only **CPAs** (Certified Public Accountants), licensed by the state, can conduct the audits.

- **Ethical behavior** is defined by the **AICPA's** (American Institute of CPA's) Code of Professional Conduct. This code holds CPAs accountable for serving the public interest.

- The five full-time members of the **Public Company Accounting Oversight Board** establish auditing standards and conduct inspections of the public accounting firms that perform audits.

Q1   (**FASB / SEC / GAAP / AICPA**) are the rules that must be followed when preparing the financial statements for external use.

Q2   **GAAP** stands for _____ _____ _____ _____ .

Q3   (**CPAs / Management / Corporate accountants**) conduct audits that attest to whether a company's financial statements comply with GAAP.

HISTORICAL COST PRINCIPLE

GAAP #1: The Historical Cost Principle states that assets and services should be recorded at their acquisition cost, therefore, using the most reliable information.

Q4   An auto has a sticker price of $20,000. A company purchases the auto, but negotiates with the sales person and pays a price of only $18,000. On the balance sheet, (**$18,000 / $20,000**) will be reported for the auto.

Q5   30 years ago land was purchased for $2,000. Now the land has a current market value of $100,000. On the balance sheet, (**$2,000 / $100,000**) will be reported for the land.

Q6   When the financial statements are prepared according to GAAP, assets and services are reported at their (**acquisition cost / current market value**).

Q7   THINK ABOUT IT: Is knowledge of an asset's current market value ever useful?   (**Yes / No**)

If so, when?

Activity 6   **ANALYSIS: RATIOS**

Purpose: ·   Understand that analysis reveals relationships
                   ·   Explore the relationships between assets, liabilities, revenues, and net income
                   ·   Examine the debt ratio, ROS (return-on-sales) ratio, asset-turnover ratio, and the ROA (return-on-asset) ratio

The **three types of analysis** are Ratio Analysis, Trend Analysis (horizontal analysis), and Common-Size Statements (vertical analysis). **Analysis reveals relationships** by comparing amounts to:
     (1)   other amounts for the same period (ratios and common-size statements),
     (2)   the same information from a prior period (trend analysis),
     (3)   competitor information, and industry norms.

RATIOS

Microsoft (MSFT), **Wal-Mart Stores** (WMT), and **Ford Motor Company** (F) are each well-known companies. But how much do you really know about them?

Q1   *FINANCIAL TRIVIA*   For the fiscal year ending before 1/31/2006, **guess** which corporation…

     a.   reports the greatest amount of assets?   **(MSFT / WMT / F)**

     b.   is financed primarily with equity rather than debt?   **(MSFT / WMT / F)**

     c.   reports the greatest amount of revenue?   **(MSFT / WMT / F)**

     d.   uses the least amount of assets to generate the greatest revenue?   **(MSFT / WMT / F)**

     e.   has the greatest overall profitability?   **(MSFT / WMT / F)**

Q2   *FINANCIAL TRIVIA*   For the fiscal year ended before 1/31/2006, **guess** what amount was reported for…

     a.   total assets of Ford Motor Company? $_____ million

     b.   total liabilities of Ford Motor Company? $_____ million

     c.   revenue of Wal-Mart Stores, Incorporated? $_____ million

     d.   net income of Wal-Mart Stores, Incorporated? $_____ million

     e.   the portion of every revenue dollar resulting in profit for Microsoft?   _____%

     f.   the portion of every revenue dollar resulting in profit for Ford Motor Company? _____%

Now turn the page and see how well you guessed.

Q3 a.   For each company listed below compute the debt ratio, which reveals the proportion of assets financed with debt. *Debt ratio = Total assets / Total liabilities*

($ in millions)	Date	Total Assets	Total Liabilities	Debt Ratio
a. Microsoft (MSFT)	6/31/2005	70,815	22,700	0.3206 or 32.06%
b. Wal-Mart Stores (WMT)	1/31/2006	138,187	85,016	
c. Ford Motor Company (F)	12/31/2005	269,476	256,519	

b.   Wal-Mart finances _____% of assets with debt. Microsoft is primarily financed with (**debt / equity**), resulting in a debt ratio that is (**less / more**) than 50%, while Ford is primarily financed with (**debt / equity**), resulting in a debt ratio that is (**less / more**) than 50%.

Q4 a.   For each company listed below compute the Return-On-Sales (ROS) ratio, which reveals the portion of each revenue dollar that results in profit. *ROS = Net income / Revenue*

($ in millions)	Year Ended	Revenue	Net Income	ROS
a. Microsoft (MSFT)	6/31/2005	39,788	12,250	0.3079 or 30.79%
b. Wal-Mart Stores (WMT)	1/31/2006	312,427	11,231	
c. Ford Motor Company (F)	12/31/2005	177,089	2,024	

b.   Ford Motor Company has (**greater /less**) revenue than Microsoft, but Ford Motor Company has a (**higher / lower**) ROS ratio than Microsoft. The ROS ratio for Microsoft indicates _____% of every revenue dollar resulted in profit (net income), but for Ford Motor Company only _____% of every revenue dollar resulted in profit.

c.   For Wal-Mart, _____ cents of each revenue dollar went to pay for all of the costs of running the business, leaving _____ cents of each revenue dollar for profit.

d.   The corporation with the strongest ROS ratio is (**MSFT / WMT / F**). How can a company increase its ROS ratio?

e.   Does a low ROS ratio indicate a weak corporation? (**Yes / No**) Why?

Q5 a.   For each company listed below compute the Asset Turnover (Asset T/O) ratio, which reveals how efficiently assets are used to generate revenue. *Asset T/O ratio = Revenue / Total assets*

($ in millions)	Year Ended	Revenue	Total Assets	Asset T/O
a. Microsoft (MSFT)	6/31/2005	39,788	70,815	0.56
b. Wal-Mart Stores (WMT)	1/31/2006	312,427	138,187	
c. Ford Motor Company (F)	12/31/2005	177,089	269,476	

b.   The asset-turnover ratios computed above are primarily in the range (**less than 3 / 3 or more**).

c.   (**MSFT / WMT / F**) has the strongest asset-turnover ratio, indicating the company makes profits by generating a large volume of revenue using relatively few assets. Wal-Mart generates $_____ in revenue for every $1 invested in assets.

Q6   **a.**   For each company listed below compute the Return-On-Asset (ROA) ratio, which reveals how efficiently assets are used to generate profit (net income). A high ROA ratio depends on managing asset investments to produce the greatest amount of revenue and controlling expenses to keep net income high. Analyze the components, ROS and Asset T/O, to better understand corporate strategy (product-differentiation vs. low-cost strategies). ROA is the broadest and best overall measure of profitability. *ROA = Net Income / Total Assets*

($ in millions)	Year Ended	Net Income	Total Assets	ROA
a. Microsoft (MSFT)	6/31/2005	12,250	70,815	0.1730 or 17.30%
b. Wal-Mart Stores (WMT)	1/31/2006	11,231	138,187	
c. Ford Motor Company (F)	12/31/2005	2,024	269,476	

b.   For each company below compute ROA by multiplying the two components, Return On Sales and Asset Turnover, previously computed. *ROA = ROS x Asset T/O*

($ in millions)	Year Ended	ROS	Asset T/O	ROA
a. Microsoft (MSFT)	6/31/2005	0.3079	.56	0.1730 or 17.30%
b. Wal-Mart Stores (WMT)	1/31/2006			
c. Ford Motor Company (F)	12/31/2005			

c.   The corporation with the strongest overall measure of profitability is (**MSFT / WMT / F**).

d.   ROA ratios computed above are in the range of (**less than 20% / 20% or more**).
The ROA for Wal-Mart indicates that every dollar invested in assets, on average, generates _____ cents in profits.

e.   Wal-Mart Stores has (**high / low**) ROS and (**high / low**) Asset T/O, indicating that a (**low-cost / product-differentiation**) strategy is used while Microsoft has (**high / low**) ROS and (**high / low**) Asset T/O, indicating that a (**low-cost / product-differentiation**) strategy is used. Ford Motor Company has (**high / low**) ROS and (**high / low**) Asset T/O, indicating that it is (**doing well / in trouble**).

Q7   **a.**   The ratio that measures the ability to translate revenue into profit is the (**Debt / ROS / Asset T/O / ROA**) ratio.

b.   The ratio that measures the proportion of debt used to finance assets is the (**Debt / ROS / Asset T/O / ROA**) ratio.

c.   The broadest measure of profitability that can be broken down into components to better understand corporate strategy is the (**Debt / ROS / Asset T/O / ROA**) ratio.

d.   A high (**Debt / ROS / Asset T/O / ROA**) ratio indicates a high-volume strategy.

Activity 7   **ANALYSIS: TREND**

Purpose: ·   Prepare a trend analysis and understand the information provided

The **TREND ANALYSIS** compares amounts of a more recent year to a base year. The base year is the earliest year being studied. The analysis measures the percentage of change from the base year.

Q1   Use the amounts listed below to complete the trend indexes for *Total expenses* and *Net income*. Divide each amount by the amount of the base year. Record the resulting *trend index* in the shaded area. Use 2002 as the base year.

PEPSICO ($ in millions)	2005	2004	2003	BASE YEAR 2002
Sales revenue	$32,562 130%	$29,261 117%	$29,971 119%	$25,112 100%
Total expenses	28,484	25,049	26,403	21,799
Net income	$4,078	$4,212	$3,568	$3,313

Q2   From 2002 to 2005 sales growth for PepsiCo was 30%, while total expenses increased _____% during the same period. When net sales increase, expenses would be expected to (**increase / stay the same / decrease**). It is favorable when sales increase by 30% and expenses increase at a (**greater / lesser**) rate than 30%. From 2002 to 2005 (**revenues / expenses**) of PepsiCo increased at a greater rate, which is (**favorable / unfavorable**).

Q3   Assume PepsiCo had a goal of increasing profits by 5% each year. This goal was (**met / not met**).

Q4   The best year financially for PepsiCo was (**2005 / 2004 / 2003**).   Why?
      The worst year financially for PepsiCo was (**2005 / 2004 / 2003**).   Why?

Q5   Use the amounts listed below to complete the trend indexes for *Liabilities* and *Stockholders' Equity*. Divide each amount by the amount for the base year. Record the resulting *trend index* in the shaded area. Use 12/31/2002 as the base year.

PEPSICO ($ in millions)	12/31/2005	12/31/2004	12/31/2003	BASE YEAR 12/31/2002
Assets	$31,727 135%	$27,987 119%	$25,327 108%	$23,474 100%
Liabilities	17,407	14,415	13,431	14,176
Stockholders' Equity	$14,320	$13,572	$11,896	$9,298

Q6   The assets of PepsiCo increased by 35% from 12/31/2002 to 12/31/2005, indicating PepsiCo is (**growing / shrinking**). From 12/31/2002 to 12/31/2005, (**assets / liabilities**) increased at a greater rate, indicating the corporation is relying (**more / less**) on debt to finance assets.

Q7   Liability amounts are greater than the base year on (**12-31-2005 / 12-31-2004 / 12-31-2003**) when the trend index is (**greater / less**) than 100. Liability amounts are less than the base year on (**12-31-2005 / 12-31-2004 / 12-31-2003**) when the trend index is (**greater / less**) than 100.

Q8   It is easier to analyze PepsiCo (**before / after**) preparing the trend analysis.

ANALYSIS: COMMON-SIZE STATEMENTS

Purpose: · Prepare common-size statements and understand the information provided

The **COMMON-SIZE INCOME STATEMENT** compares all amounts within one year to revenue of that same year. The analysis measures each income statement amount as a percentage of revenue.

Q1 For the Coca-Cola (KO) and Starbucks (SBUX) companies listed below, complete the common-size statements by dividing each amount on the income statement by sales revenue. Record the resulting common-size percentage in the shaded area provided.

($ in millions)	PEPSICO (PEP) 12/31/2005		COCA-COLA (KO) 12/31/2005		STARBUCKS (SBUX) 10/2/2005	
Sales revenue	$32,562	100%	$23,104		$6,369	
Total expenses	28,484	87%	18,232		5,874	
Net income	$4,078	13%	$4,872		$495	

Q2 **(PEP / KO / SBUX)** is the largest company above reporting sales revenue of approximately $32 **(trillion / billion / million / thousand)**. ROS for PepsiCo is _____% or ___._____ in decimal form, which indicates _____ cents of every dollar of sales revenue resulted in profit. Return-on-sales ratio *(ROS) = Net income / Revenue*

Q3 On the common-size income statement, every amount is compared to or divided by total (**assets / liabilities / revenue / net income**). Common-size statements are helpful when comparing companies of different size. (**True / False**)

Q4 Based only on the information provided above, which company would be your choice of investment? (**PEP / KO / SBUX**) *Why?*

The **COMMON-SIZE BALANCE SHEET** compares all amounts within one year to total assets of that same year. The analysis measures each balance sheet amount as a percentage of total assets.

Q5 For the Coca-Cola (KO) and Starbucks (SBUX) companies listed below, complete the common-size statements by dividing each amount on the balance sheet by total assets. Record the resulting common-size percentage in the shaded area provided.

($ in millions)	PEPSICO (PEP) 12/31/2005		COCA-COLA (KO) 12/31/2005		STARBUCKS (SBUX) 10/2/2005	
Assets	$70,444	100%	$68,144		$42,141	
Liabilities	$17,407	25%	$13,072		$1,423	
Stockholders' Equity	$53,037	75%	$55,072		$40,718	

Q6 Starbucks primarily finances assets with (**liabilities / stockholders' equity**). The debt ratio for Starbucks is _____%, which indicates debt (liabilities) is used to finance _____% of assets and equity (stockholders' equity) is used to finance _____% of assets. *Debt Ratio = Liabilities / Assets*. On the common-size balance sheet, every amount is compared to or divided by total (**assets / liabilities / revenue / net income**).

COCA-COLA (KO*)   12/31/2005 BALANCE SHEET   ($ in millions)

ASSETS		LIABILITIES	
Cash and cash equivalents	$ 4,701	Accounts payable	$ 5,290
Short-term investments	66	Short-term debt	4,546
Accounts receivable, net	2,281	Other current liabilities	0
Inventories	1,424	Long-term debt	1,154
Other current assets	1,778	Other non-current liabilities	2,082
Property, plant, and equipment, net	5,786		
		STOCKHOLDERS' EQUITY	
Goodwill	1,047		
Other intangibles	2,774	Contributed capital	6,369
Long-term investments	6,922	Retained earnings	31,299
Other non-current assets	2,648	Other stockholders' equity	(21,313)
TOTAL ASSETS	**$29,427**	**TOTAL L & SE**	**$29,427**

COCA-COLA (KO)   2005 INCOME STATEMENT   ($ in millions)

Sales revenue	$23,104
Cost of goods sold	7,263
Gross profit	15,841
Selling, general, and administrative expense	8,824
Depreciation and amortization expense	932
Other revenues and expenses	605
Income before income tax	6,690
Provision for income tax	1,818
Net income	$ 4,872

COCA-COLA (KO)   2005 STATEMENT OF RETAINED EARNINGS   ($ in millions)

Retained earnings, beginning	$29,105
+ Net income (earnings of this accounting period)	4,872
- Dividends (earnings distributed to shareholders)	(2,678)
= Retained earnings, ending	$31,299

COCA-COLA (KO)   2005 STATEMENT OF CASH FLOWS   ($ in millions)

Net cash from operating activities (NCOA)	$6,423
Net cash from investing activities (NCIA)	(1,496)
Net cash from financing activities (NCFA)	(6,785)
Effect of exchange rate changes	(148)
Change in cash	(2,006)
+ Cash, beginning of the period	6,707
= Cash, end of the period	$4,701

TEST YOUR UNDERSTANDING

Purpose: · Review the four financial statements
           · Compute net income
           · Prepare and evaluate trend and common-size statements

Q1 *Review the 2005 Financial Statements of the Coca-Cola Company on the opposite page to answer the following questions*:

 a.   Is the accounting equation in balance? (**Yes / No**)
      Assets $_____ million = Liabilities $_____ million + SE $_____ million
 b.   What amount of sales revenue was earned? $_____ million
 c.   The title of the largest expense account is _____ reporting $_____ million.
 d.   Was the company profitable? (**Yes / No**)
 e.   Did the company declare dividends? (**Yes / No**)
 f.   Was there an increase in cash during the accounting period? (**Yes / No**)

 g.   Net income of $_____ million is reported on the Income Statement. It is also reported on the (**Statement of Retained Earnings / Balance Sheet / Statement of Cash Flows**).

 h.   The amount reported for the ending balance of retained earnings on the Statement of Retained Earnings is $_____ million. It is also reported on the (**Income Statement / Balance Sheet / Statement of Cash Flows**).

 i.   The amount reported for cash on the Balance Sheet is $_____ million. It is also reported on the (**Income Statement / Statement of Retained Earnings / Statement of Cash Flows**).

Q2 Make the following statements true by correcting the false information. Some statements may need more than one correction. Note: *There may be more than one way to correct the false information.*

 a.   The four financial statements include the revenue statement, statement of retained earnings, long-term liabilities statement, and the statement of cash flows.

 b.   The statement of cash flows reports the assets of the business and how those assets are financed.

 c.   Assets are financed either by liabilities or expenses.

 d.   Retained earnings is an asset account, accounts receivable is a liability account, and accounts payable is a stockholders' equity account.

 e.   Accounts receivable are amounts to be paid later to suppliers by the corporation.

 f.   Wages payable reported on the balance sheet is the cost of labor for the entire accounting period.

 g.   The income statement reports cash inflows and cash outflows.

 h.   Cash is the amount earned engaging in the primary business activity.

 i.   When a dentist provides services to a patient, a gain is reported on the income statement.

 j.   Earnings is another term for revenue.

 k.   Net income distributed to shareholders is referred to as contributed capital.

 l.   Dividends are reported as an expense on the income statement.

Q3 Circle the income statement accounts below. Next, compute net income.

Supply expense	$ 8,000
Notes payable	30,000
Cost of goods sold	75,000
Sales revenue	100,000
Common stock	50,000
Dividends	2,000

Q4 20X1 was the first year of business. During the year, $100,000 of wage costs were incurred; $95,000 were paid in cash to employees; and the remaining $5,000 of wages will be paid to employees on January 3 of the coming year, the next payday. What account title and amount will be reported on each of the following year-end financial statements?

a. 20X1 Income Statement   Account title: Wage _____ of $_____

b. 12/31/20X1 Balance Sheet   Account title: Wages _____ of $_____

c. 20X1 Statement of Cash Flows Account title: Wages _____ of $_____

Q5 THINK ABOUT IT   Are Generally Accepted Accounting Principles (GAAP) necessary? **(Yes / No)** Why or why not?

Q6 For the Coca-Cola Company listed below, complete the trend indexes for *Total expenses* and *Net income*. Record the resulting *trend index* in the shaded area. Use 2002 as the base year.

Coca-Cola (KO) ($ in millions)	2005		2004		2003		BASE YEAR 2002	
Sales revenue	$23,104	118%	$21,962	112%	$21,044	108%	$19,564	100%
Total expenses	18,232		17,115		16,697		16,514	
Net income	$4,872		$4,847		$4,347		$3,050	

From 2002 to 2005 sales revenue of Coca-Cola increased by _____%, while expenses increased by _____%, resulting in an increase in net income of _____%. Coca-Cola has done a **(poor / okay / spectacular)** job of controlling expenses, resulting in a **(poor / okay / spectacular)** net income.

Q7 For the Coca-Cola Company, complete the common-size statements for 12/31/2002, 12/31/2003, and 12/31/2004 below. Record the resulting *common-size %* in the shaded area provided.

Coca-Cola (KO) ($ in millions)	12/31/2005		12/31/2004		12/31/2003		12/31/2002	
Assets	$29,427	100%	$31,327		$27,342		$24,501	
Liabilities	$13,072	44%	$15,392		$13,252		$12,701	
Stockholders' Equity	$16,355	56%	$15,935		$14,090		$11,800	

On 12/31/2002 this company primarily financed assets with **(liabilities / stockholders' equity)** and on 12/31/2005 assets were primarily financed with **(liabilities / stockholders' equity)**, indicating that on 12/31/2005 this company is relying **(more / less)** on debt to finance assets. In the common-size *balance sheet*, every amount is compared to or divided by _____. In the common-size *income statement*, every amount is compared to or divided by _____.

CHAPTER 2 – BALANCE SHEET

Activity 10   THE CLASSIFIED BALANCE SHEET

Purpose: · Identify account classifications typically used on the balance sheet

STARBUCKS (SBUX)	10/2/2005 BALANCE SHEET		($ in millions)
ASSETS		**LIABILITIES**	
Cash and cash equivalents	$ 173.8	Accounts payable	$ 221.0
Short-term investments	133.2	Short-term debt	277.7
Accounts receivable	190.8	Other current liabilities	728.3
Inventories	546.3	Long-term debt	2.9
Other current assets	165.2	Other non-current liabilities	193.6
PPE, net	1,842.0	**STOCKHOLDERS' EQUITY**	
Goodwill	92.0	Contributed capital	130.4
Long-term investments	262.0	Retained earnings	1,939.4
Other non-current assets	108.8	Other stockholders' equity	20.8
TOTAL ASSETS	**$3,514.1**	**TOTAL L & SE**	**$3,514.1**

A classified balance sheet breaks the three major account types (assets, liabilities, and stockholders' equity) into smaller classifications to help decision makers better understand the information presented. Following are typical classifications and a brief description.

- **Current assets** (CA) are expected to be converted into cash, sold, or consumed within twelve months.
- **Property, plant, and equipment** (PPE) summarize amounts for equipment, buildings, and land. These are long-term assets that are expected to benefit more than one accounting period. **Depreciation expense** is the cost allocated to each year of the asset's useful life. **Accumulated depreciation** is the total amount of depreciation expensed since the asset's date of purchase. Acquisition cost – accumulated depreciation = the **book value** of PPE, which is the amount added to compute total assets on the balance sheet. Land is not depreciated.
- **Other assets** include other long-term asset accounts such as **Investments** and **Intangible Assets**.
- **Current liabilities** (CL) are amounts owed to creditors that are expected to be repaid within twelve months. Examples include accounts payable and short-term debt.
- **Long-term liabilities** (LTL) are amounts owed to creditors that are expected to be repaid in more than twelve months. Examples include bonds payable and long-term debt.
- **Contributed capital** (CC) includes amounts paid (contributed) by stockholders to purchase common stock and preferred stock. Accounts include common stock and additional-paid-in capital (APIC).
- **Retained earnings** (RE) is net income earned by the company since its incorporation and not yet distributed as dividends.
- **Other stockholders' equity** includes treasury stock and adjustments to stockholders' equity such as the change in value of long-term investments.

To answer the following questions refer to the balance sheet presented above.

Q1   How many of the accounts listed are Current Assets? (**1 / 3 / 5**)
       Property, Plant, and Equipment? (**1 / 3 / 5**)   Other Assets? (**1 / 3 / 5**)

Q2   What would be the total amount reported for Current Liabilities? $_____ million;
       Long-term Liabilities? $_____ million; Total Stockholders' Equity? $_____ million

UNDERSTANDING THE BALANCE SHEET

Purpose:
- Identify the value at which amounts are reported on the balance sheet
- Understand what an increase or a decrease in an account indicates
- Develop strategies for analyzing the balance sheet

STARBUCKS (SBUX) BALANCE SHEET ($ in millions)				
ASSETS	**10/2/2005**	**10/3/2004**	**9/28/2003**	**9/29/2002**
Cash and cash equivalents	$ 173.8	$ 299.1	$ 200.9	$ 99.7
Short-term investments	133.2	353.9	149.1	227.7
Accounts receivable	190.8	140.2	114.4	97.6
Inventories	546.3	422.7	342.9	263.2
Other current assets	165.2	135.0	102.7	84.4
Property, plant, and equipment	3,467.6	2,877.7	2,516.3	2,080.2
Accumulated depreciation	(1,625.6)	(1,326.3)	(1,068.6)	(814.4)
PPE, net	1,842.0	1,551.4	1,447.7	1,265.8
Goodwill	92.0	69.0	63.3	19.9
Long-term investments	262.0	306.9	280.4	102.5
Other non-current assets	108.8	112.3	77.1	53.6
TOTAL ASSETS	**$3,514.1**	**$3,390.5**	**$2,778.5**	**$2,214.4**
LIABILITIES				
Accounts payable	$ 221.0	$ 199.3	$ 169.0	$ 136.0
Short-term debt	277.7	0.7	0.7	0.7
Other current liabilities	728.3	546.1	404.5	325.9
Long-term debt	2.9	3.6	4.4	5.1
Other non-current liabilities	193.6	166.4	128.8	**(L)**
STOCKHOLDERS' EQUITY				
Contributed capital	130.4	996.1	998.5	930.4
Retained earnings	1,939.4	1,448.9	1,058.3	801.3
Other stockholders' equity	20.8	29.4	14.3	(9.0)
TOTAL L & SE	**$3,514.1**	**$3,390.5**	**$2,778.5**	**$ (Z)**

Q1 **Use the balance sheet dated 10/2/2005 above to answer the following questions:**

a. How much do customers owe this company? $_____ million

b. For *inventories*, $546.3 million is the (**acquisition cost** / current market value / book value / can't tell).

c. For *property, plant and equipment, net*, $1,842.0 million is the (acquisition cost / current market value / **book value** / can't tell).

d. What amount of *investments* does this company intend to hold for more than a year?
$_____ million

e. How much does this company owe to suppliers? $_____ million

f. *Contributed capital* amounts represent the (**amount paid-in** / market / book / present) value.

g. Starbucks is relying most heavily on (debt / contributed capital / retained earnings) to finance assets.

h. The balance sheet reports a company's financial position (**as of a certain date** / **over a period of time**).

i. Assets and liabilities are recorded on the balance sheet in order of (**magnitude** / **alphabetically** / **liquidity**), which means that (**PPE** / **cash**) should be listed before (**PPE** / **cash**).

Q2 *Use the balance sheets on the previous page to answer the following questions:*

a. Calculate the amounts that should be reported for (Z) and (L) on the 9/29/2002 balance sheet:
(Z) = $_____ million   (L) = $_____ million

b. What was the beginning balance of the *inventories* account for the fiscal year ended on
10/2/2005? $_____ million   10/3/2004? $_____ million   9/28/2003? $_____ million

c. What amount of *property, plant, and equipment* was purchased during the fiscal year ended on
10/2/2005? $_____ million   10/3/2004? $_____ million   9/28/2003? $_____ million

d. *Long-term debt* was paid back during fiscal years ending in (**2005** / **2004** / **2003**). In general, this trend indicates (**more** / **less**) financial risk. As of 10/2/2005 this company owes long-term debt of
$_____ million to creditors.

Q3 *Use the balance sheets on the previous page to answer the following questions:*

a. *Total Assets* are (**increasing** / **decreasing**), indicating this company is (**expanding** / **shrinking**).

b. From 9/29/2002 to 9/28/2003 the *Contributed Capital* account (**increased** / **decreased**), indicating the company (**issued more stock** / **purchased more assets** / **reported net income**) of $_____ million during this accounting period.

c. *Retained Earnings* is (**increasing** / **decreasing**), indicating this company is
(**issuing more stock** / **purchasing more assets** / **reporting net income**).
Assuming no dividends were issued, how much *net income (loss)* was reported for the fiscal year ended
on 10/2/2005? $_____ million   10/3/2004? $_____ million   9/28/2003? $_____ million

The most profitable year was during the fiscal year ending in (**2005** / **2004** / **2003**).

d. Develop a strategy to analyze the balance sheet. Which line would you look at first? Second? Third?
Explain why.

e. Review the series of balance sheets. This company appears to report a (**strong** / **weak**) financial position. Support your response with at least two observations.

DEBT vs. EQUITY

Purpose: · Identify the characteristics of debt and equity
· Assess financial risk

Corporations externally finance the purchase of assets with debt (liabilities) or equity (common stock).

Assets = Liabilities + Stockholders' Equity

Large amounts of **debt** are usually issued in the form of bonds. The borrowing corporation records bonds payable and is referred to as the *debtor* and the entity loaning the money records a bond receivable and is referred to as the *creditor*. The debtor must pay back the amount borrowed plus interest to the creditor. The interest paid by the borrowing corporation is an expense that reduces taxable income. The return to creditors is the interest received. Creditors are not owners of the corporation, and therefore, have no ownership rights.

Equity refers to the issuance of stock, which may be common stock or preferred stock. Entities owning shares of stock are the owners of the corporation and are referred to as *stockholders* or shareholders. Stockholder's primary ownership rights include a right to vote at annual meetings and a right to a portion of the profits (net income). *Dividends* are the distribution of profits to stockholders. The corporate board of directors decides whether to pay dividends or not and has no obligation to purchase the shares of stock back from the stockholders. If stockholders sell their shares of stock, they usually sell to another investor using a stockbroker, who in turn executes the trade on a stock exchange such as the New York Stock Exchange or NASDAQ. Stockholders earn a return on their investment by receiving dividends or selling the stock for a greater amount than the purchase price.

The balance sheet helps investors, both creditors and stockholders, assess the degree of financial risk a corporation is assuming. In general, the more a corporation relies on debt to finance assets, the greater the financial risk of the corporation.

$ in millions 12/31/2005	Google (GOOG)	General Motors (GM)
Assets	$10,272	$ (Y)
Liabilities	$ 853	$448,239
Stockholders' equity	$ (B)	$ 15,425
Debt ratio	%	%

Q1   Compute the values for (B) and (Y) in the above chart. Compute the **Debt Ratio** and record in the above chart. This ratio quantifies the proportion of assets financed with debt. *Debt ratio = Liabilities / Assets*
(**Google / GM**) is financing assets primarily with debt; therefore, (**Google / GM**) is assuming the greater financial risk. Based only on the information presented above, which company would you choose as an investment? (**Google / GM**) Why?

Q2   For each item circle the correct response when comparing the issuance of debt and equity.
a.   The corporation (**has to / does not have to**) pay interest to creditors, but (**has to / does not have to**) pay dividends to shareholders.
b.   The corporation (**must / never has to**) repay amounts borrowed from creditors, but (**must / never has to**) repay amounts invested by shareholders.
c.   The interest expense of debt (**reduces / does not reduce**) taxable income, but dividends paid to shareholders (**reduce / do not reduce**) taxable income.
d.   Issuing additional debt (**does / does not**) dilute shareholder's ownership rights, but issuing additional shares of common stock (**does / does not**) dilute shareholder's ownership rights.
e.   If you were the CFO of a *large* company, how would you recommend financing assets? Primarily with (**debt / equity**). Why? If this was a *small* company? Primarily with (**debt / equity**). Why?

ANALYSIS: RATIOS

Purpose: · Understand the information provided by the current ratio and the debt ratio

Liquidity and Solvency Ratios measure the ability to meet financial obligations and the level of financial risk.

The **Current Ratio** measures the ability to pay current payables as they come due by comparing current assets to current liabilities. It is a measure of short-term liquidity. A higher ratio indicates a stronger ability to pay current debts.

$$\text{Current Ratio} = \frac{\text{Current assets}}{\text{Current liabilities}}$$

The **Debt Ratio** measures the proportion of assets financed by debt by comparing total liabilities to total assets. It is a measure of long-term solvency. A higher ratio indicates greater financial risk.

$$\text{Debt Ratio} = \frac{\text{Total liabilities}}{\text{Total assets}}$$

	Current Ratio	Debt Ratio	**Debt-to-Equity Ratio
Industry average for retail-eating places	*1.10*	*0.38*	*0.62*
Applebee's (APPB)	0.60	0.32	0.46
Darden Restaurants (DRI)	0.50	0.34	0.52
Landry's Restaurants (LNY)	0.60	0.61	1.59

Use the chart immediately above to answer the following questions. Stock symbols are shown in parentheses.

Q1   Of the above three restaurant chains, which is your favorite? (APPB / DRI / LNY)
    APPB operates Applebee's Neighborhood Grill & Bar.
    DRI operates Red Lobster, Olive Garden, Bahama Breeze, and Smokey Bones Barbeque and Grill.
    LYN operates Joe's Crab Shack, Rainforest Café, Landry's Seafood House, and The Crab House.

Q2   Current liabilities are usually paid off with current assets. A current ratio that is (lower / higher) than the industry average may indicate a lack of short-term liquidity, which includes (APPB / DRI / LNY). Does this indicate that these corporations are insolvent or unable to pay their bills? (Yes / No) *Explain.*

Q3   (APPB / DRI / LNY) are relying more on debt to finance assets and have a debt ratio (greater / less) than 0.50. Darden Restaurants is financing _____% of assets with debt. For a company wanting to be lower risk and less dependent on debt, a(n) (increasing / decreasing) trend in the debt ratio is considered favorable. A company that has higher financial risk will, in general, be required to pay (higher / lower) interest rates when borrowing money.

Q4   Why does a company with a greater debt ratio tend to be a higher financial risk?

Q5   Does a high debt ratio indicate a weak corporation? (Yes / No) *Explain* your answer.

** *Some financial sources report the Debt-to-Equity ratio that describes the same information as the Debt Ratio but in a different format. Debt ratio = Debt-to-equity ratio / (1 + debt-to-equity ratio). For Applebee's 0.32 = 0.46/1.46*

ANALYSIS: TREND

Purpose:　　　· Prepare a trend analysis and understand the information provided

A TREND ANALYSIS compares amounts of a more recent year to a base year. The base year is the earliest year being studied. The analysis measures the percentage of change from the base year.

Q1　For Starbucks, use the amounts listed below to compute the trend indexes for long-term liabilities (LTL), common stock (CS), and retained earnings (RE) by dividing each amount by the amount for the base year. Record the resulting *trend index* in the shaded area. Use 9/29/2002 as the base year.

STARBUCKS ($ in millions)	10/2/2005 Amount	Trend Index	10/3/2004 Amount	Trend Index	9/28/2003 Amount	Trend Index	9/29/2002 BASE YEAR	
Current assets	$1,209.3	157	$1,350.9	175	$ 910.0	118	$ 772.6	100
PPE, net	1,842.0	146	1,551.4	123	1,447.7	114	1,265.8	100
Other assets	462.8	263	488.2	277	420.8	239	176.0	100
TOTAL ASSETS	$3,514.1	159	$3,390.5	153	$2,778.5	125	$2,214.4	100
Current liabilities	$1,227.0	265	$ 746.1	161	$ 574.2	124	$ 462.6	100
Long-term liabilities	196.5	___	170.0	___	133.2	___	29.1	___
Common stock	130.4		996.1		998.5		930.4	
Retained earnings	1,939.4	___	1,448.9	___	1,058.3	___	801.3	___
Other SE	20.8	*NA	29.4	*NA	14.3	*NA	(9.0)	100
TOTAL L and SE	$3,514.1	159	$3,390.5	153	$2,778.5	125	$2,214.4	100

Amounts with opposite signs cannot be accurately compared.

Refer to the series of balance sheets and the trend analysis above to answer the following questions.

Q2　A trend index of 159 indicates that the dollar amount is (**greater** / **less**) than the (**previous** / **base**) year, while a trend index of 14 indicates the dollar amount is (**greater** / **less**) than the (**previous** / **base**) year. For *total assets*, the trend index of 159 is computed by dividing $3,514.1 (total assets on 10/2/20005) by $_____ (total assets of the base year). A trend index of 159 indicates *total assets* (**increased** / **decreased**) by _____% (from an index of 100 to 159) from 9/29/2002 to 10/02/2005.

Q3　From 9/29/2002 to 10/02/2005, which of the following accounts increased at a greater rate than total assets? (**LTL** / **CS** / **RE**). This indicates that in the latter years the company is relying more on (**LTL** / **CS** / **RE**) to finance assets and less on (**LTL** / **CS** / **RE**) to finance assets.

Q4　The rate of annual total asset growth can be compared between companies.
　　　Assume less than 5% is low, 5-15% is moderate, and over 15% is high.
　　　The *average* rate of annual total asset growth from 9/29/2002 to 10/02/2005 is (**low** / **moderate** / **high**).

Q5　Examine the financial information reported above and comment on at least two items of significance that the trend analysis helps to reveal.

ANALYSIS: COMMON-SIZE STATEMENTS

Purpose: · Prepare common-size statements and understand the information provided

Q1 Review the balance sheet information presented below for the three restaurant chains and comment on at least two items of significance that your examination reveals.

The **COMMON-SIZE BALANCE SHEET** compares all amounts to total assets of that same year. The analysis measures each item as a percentage of total assets.

Q2 For Applebee's and Landry's Restaurants listed below, complete the common-size statements by dividing each item on the balance sheet by the amount of total assets. Record the resulting common-size percentage in the shaded area provided.

(Hint: Percentages for CA + PPE, net + Other = 100% and CL + LTL + CS + RE + Other = 100 %.)

($ in millions)	Applebee's APPB 3/26/2006 Amount	CS%	Darden Restaurants DRI 2/26/2006 Amount	CS%	Landry's Restaurants LNY 3/31/2006 Amount	CS%
Current assets	$ 80.4	%	$ 434.2	14.3%	$ 153.3	%
PPE, net	607.7	%	2,408.9	79.5%	1,421.0	%
Other assets	200.0	%	187.3	6.2%	97.9	%
TOTAL ASSETS	**$888.1**	%	**$3,030.4**	**100.0%**	**$1,672.2**	%
Current liabilities	$142.7	%	$ 868.6	28.7%	$ 241.5	%
Long-term liabilities	296.9	%	911.9	30.1%	906.9	%
Common stock	1.1	%	1,796.1	59.3%	0.2	%
Retained earnings	737.4	%	1,621.8	53.5%	204.2	%
Other SE	(290.0)	%	(2,168.0)	(71.5)%	319.4	%
TOTAL L and SE	**$888.1**	%	**$3,030.4**	**100.0%**	**$1,672.2**	%

* Note: The percentages may not sum to 100% due to rounding error.

Refer to the series of balance sheets and the common-size analysis above to answer the following questions.

Q3 The debt ratio (Total liabilities / Total assets) for Darden Restaurants is _____ % or ___._____ (decimal form).

Q4 The assets of (APPB / DRI / LNY) are most heavily financed with *borrowed* amounts.
Q5 The assets of (APPB / DRI / LNY) are most heavily financed with amounts *invested by shareholders.*
Q6 The assets of (APPB / DRI / LNY) are most heavily financed with *past profits.*

Q7 Review the balance sheet information presented above for the three restaurant chains and comment on at least two items of significance that the common-size statements help to reveal.

Q8 Were these companies easier to compare before or after you prepared the common-size statements? (Before / After) Why?

ANALYSIS of YUM! BRANDS

Purpose: ·Understand and interpret amounts reported on the balance sheet

YUM! BRANDS (YUM)   BALANCE SHEET   ($ in millions)

ASSETS	12/31/2005	12/31/2004	12/31/2003	12/31/2002
Cash and cash equivalents	$ 158	$ 62	$ 192	$ 130
Short-term investments	43	54	15	27
Accounts receivable	236	192	150	168
Inventories	85	76	67	63
Other current assets	315	363	382	342
Property, plant, and equipment	6,186	6,057	5,606	5,201
Accumulated depreciation	(2,830)	(2,618)	(2,326)	(2,164)
PPE, net	3,356	3,439	3,280	3,037
Goodwill	538	553	521	485
Long-term investments	173	194	184	229
Other non-current assets	794	763	829	919
TOTAL ASSETS	**$5,698**	**$5,696**	**$5,620**	**$5,400**
LIABILITIES				
Accounts payable	$ 751	$ 1,160	$ 1,157	$ 1,166
Short-term debt	211	11	10	146
Other current liabilities	643	205	294	208
Long-term debt	1,649	1,731	2,056	2,299
Other non-current liabilities	995	994	983	987
STOCKHOLDERS' EQUITY				
Contributed capital	0	659	916	1,046
Retained earnings	1,619	1,067	414	(203)
Other stockholders' equity	(170)	(131)	(210)	(249)
TOTAL L & SE	**$5,698**	**$5,696**	**$5,620**	**$5,400**

YUM! BRANDS (YUM)   Classified Balance Sheet / Common-size Statements   ($ in millions)

	12/31/2005		12/31/2004		12/31/2003		12/31/2002	
	Amount	CS%	Amount	CS%	Amount	CS%	Amount	CS%
Current assets	$	%	$	%	$ 806.0	14.3%	$ 730.0	13.5%
PPE, net		%		%	3,280.0	58.4%	3,037.0	56.2%
Other assets		%		%	1,534.0	27.3%	1,633.0	30.2%
TOTAL ASSETS	$	%	$	%	$5,620.0	100.0%	$5,400.0	100.0%
Current liabilities		%		%	$1,461.0	26.0%	$1,520.0	28.1%
Long-term liabilities		%		%	3,039.0	54.1%	3,286.0	60.9%
TOTAL Liabilities	$	%	$	%	$4,500.0	80.1%	$4,806.0	89.0%
Contributed capital		%		%	916.0	16.3%	1,046.0	19.4%
Retained earnings		%		%	414.0	7.4%	(203.0)	(3.8)%
Other SE		%		%	(210.0)	(3.7)%	(249.0)	(4.6)%
TOTAL SE	$	%	$	%	$1,120.0	19.9%	$ 594.0	11.0%

YUM! BRANDS (YUM)   RATIOS

	Industry Norm	12/31/2005	12/31/2004	12/31/2003	12/31/2002
Current ratio	1.10			0.55	0.48
Debt ratio	0.38			0.80	0.89

Refer to the series of balance sheets for Yum! Brands (on the previous page) to answer the following questions.

Q1   YUM! Brands is the largest restaurant chain when measured by (**sales / # of units**) and operates more than 34,000 restaurants in more than 100 countries. Which is your favorite YUM! Brands restaurant? (**KFC / Pizza Hut / Taco Bell / Long John Silver's / A&W**)
Hint: Refer to company descriptions in Appendix A – Featured Corporations

Q2   *Total Assets* increased by $_____ million since 12/31/2002, an increase of _____%, which is the result of (**purchasing additional assets / issuing more common stock / increasing net income**).

Q3   In regard to assets, this company has a major investment in (**inventory / PPE / financial securities**).

Q4   On 12/31/2002, the retained earnings account reports a (**positive / negative**) amount, which is most likely the result of previously (**selling assets / purchasing treasury stock / incurring net losses on the income statement**).

Q5   This company distributed dividends for the first time during 2004, distributing $58 million in 2004 and $123 million in 2005. Use this information to compute net income for:
2005 $_____ million;   2004 $_____ million;   2003 $_____ million

Q6   For 12/31/2004 and 12/31/2005 complete the classified balance sheet by adding the items within each classification. Record your results in the area provided on the previous page. Classified balance sheets for 12/31/2002 and 12/31/2003 have already been completed.
(Hint: Amounts for CA + PPE, net + Other = Total Assets and CL + LTL + CS + RE + Other = Total L + SE.)

Q7   For 12/31/2004 and 12/31/2005 complete the common-size statements by dividing each item on the balance sheet by the amount of total assets for the same year. Record your results in the area provided on the previous page. Common-size statements for 12/31/2002 and 12/31/2003 have already been completed. *(Hint: Percentages for CA + PPE, net + Other = 100% and CL + LTL + CS + RE + Other = 100%.)*

Q8   For 12/31/2004 and 12/31/2005 compute the current ratio and the debt ratio. Record your results in the area provided on the previous page. Ratios for 12/31/2002 and 12/31/2003 have already been computed. *Comment* on the results.

Q9   On 12/31/2005 this company is relying more heavily on (**contributed capital / retained earnings**) to finance assets, while on 12/31/2002, it was relying more heavily on (**contributed capital / retained earnings**) to finance assets. Review the debt ratio. What does the debt ratio reveal about the financing of this company?

Q10   Review the financial information of this company and *comment* on

   a.   signs of financial strength.

   b.   warning signs or signs of financial weakness.

Q11   If you had $10,000, would you consider investing in this company? (**Yes / No**) Why?

ANALYSIS of MCDONALD'S

Purpose: · Understand and interpret amounts reported on the balance sheet

McDONALD'S (MCD) BALANCE SHEET ($ in millions)				
ASSETS	**12/31/2005**	**12/31/2004**	**12/31/2003**	**12/31/2002**
Cash and cash equivalents	$ 4,260.4	$ 1,379.8	$ 492.8	$ 330.4
Accounts receivable	795.9	745.5	734.5	855.3
Inventories	147.0	147.5	129.4	111.7
Other current assets	646.4	585.0	528.7	418.0
Property, plant, and equipment	29,897.2	30,507.8	28,740.2	26,218.6
Accumulated depreciation	(9,989.2)	(9,804.7)	(8,815.5)	(7,635.2)
PPE, net	19,908.0	20,703.1	19,924.7	18,583.4
Goodwill	1,950.7	1,828.3	1,665.1	1,558.5
Long-term investments	1,035.4	1,109.9	1,089.6	1,037.7
Other non-current assets	1,245.0	1,338.4	1,273.2	1,075.5
TOTAL ASSETS	**$29,988.8**	**$27,837.5**	**$25,838.0**	**$23,970.5**
LIABILITIES				
Accounts payable	$ 689.4	$ 714.3	$ 577.4	$ 635.8
Short-term debt	1,202.7	862.2	388.0	275.8
Other current liabilities	2,144.2	1,944.0	1,783.1	1,510.7
Long-term debt	8,937.4	8,357.3	9,342.5	9,703.6
Other non-current liabilities	1,869.0	1,758.2	1,765.1	1,563.7
STOCKHOLDERS' EQUITY				
Common stock, par	16.6	16.6	16.6	16.6
Additional paid-in capital	2,797.6	2,186.0	1,837.5	1,747.3
Retained earnings	23,516.0	21,755.8	20,172.3	19,204.4
Treasury stock	(10,373.6)	(9,578.1)	(9,318.5)	(8,987.7)
Other stockholders' equity	(810.5)	(178.8)	(726.0)	(1,699.7)
TOTAL L & SE	**$29,988.8**	**$27,837.5**	**$25,838.0**	**$23,970.5**

McDONALD'S Classified Balance Sheet / Trend Analysis ($ in millions)								
	12/31/2005		**12/31/2004**		**12/31/2003**		**12/31/2002**	
	Amount	Trend Index	Amount	Trend Index	Amount	Trend Index	BASE YEAR	
Current assets	$		$		$ 1,885.4	110	$ 1,715.4	100
PPE, net					19,924.7	107	18,583.4	100
Other assets					4,027.9	110	3,671.7	100
TOTAL Assets	$		$		$25,838.0	108	$23,970.5	100
Current liabilities					$ 2,748.5	113	$ 2,422.3	100
LTerm liabilities					11,107.6	99	11,267.3	100
TOTAL Liabilities	$		$		$13,856.1	101	$13,689.6	100
Contributed capital					$ 1,854.1	105	$ 1,763.9	100
Retained earnings					20,172.3	105	19,204.4	100
Other SE					(10,044.5)	94	(10,687.4)	100
TOTAL SE	$		$		$11,981.9	117	$10,280.9	100

McDONALD'S (MCD) RATIOS					
	Industry Norm	**12/31/2005**	**12/31/2004**	**12/31/2003**	**12/31/2002**
Current ratio	*1.10*			0.69	0.71
Debt ratio	*0.38*			0.54	0.57

Refer to the series of balance sheets for McDonald's on the previous page to answer the following questions.

Q1   McDonald's is the world's (**#1** / **#2**) restaurant chain when measured by (**sales** / **# of units**) and has over 31,000 restaurants in more than 100 countries. It also operates Boston Market and Chipotle Mexican Grill restaurants. *Hint: Refer to company descriptions in Appendix A – Featured Corporations*

Q2   *Total Assets* increased by $_____ million since 12/31/2002, an increase of _____%, averaging _____% per year, which is the result of (**purchasing additional assets** / **issuing more common stock** / **increasing net income**).

Q3   In regard to assets, this company has a major investment in (**inventory** / **PPE** / **financial securities**). On average, the PPE has been used for (**more** / **less**) than half of its useful life.

Q4   *Long-term debt* was paid back during (**2005** / **2004** / **2003**).

Q5   This company was able to attract new shareholders during (**2005** / **2004** / **2003**). As of 12/31/2005 shareholders have contributed a total of $_____ million to this corporation.

Q6   Additional *treasury stock* was acquired during (**2005** / **2004** / **2003**). Treasury stock results from (**selling assets** / **refinancing debt** / **repurchasing common stock**).

Q7   This company distributed dividends of $503.5 in 2003, $695 million in 2004, and $842 million in 2005. Use this information to compute net income for:
     2005 $_____ million;   2004 $_____ million;   2003 $_____ million

Q8   For 12/31/2004 and 12/31/2005 complete the classified balance sheet by adding the accounts within each classification. Record your results in the area provided on the previous page. Classified balance sheets for 12/31/2002 and 12/31/2003 have already been completed.
     (Hint: Amounts for CA + PPE, net + Other = Total Assets and CL + LTL + CS + RE + Other = Total L + SE)

Q9   For 12/31/2004 and 12/31/2005 complete the trend analysis by dividing each amount by the amount for the base year of 12/31/2002. Record the resulting *trend index* in the area provided on the previous page. For 12/31/2002 and 12/31/2003 the trend indexes have already been computed.
     Comment on at least two items of significance the trend analysis helps to reveal.

Q10   For 12/31/2004 and 12/31/2005 compute the current ratio and the debt ratio. Record your results in the area provided on the previous page. Ratios for 12/31/2002 and 12/31/2003 have already been computed. *Comment* on the results.

Q11   The assets of this company are most heavily financed with (**liabilities** / **contributed capital** / **retained earnings**). This is referred to as (**internal** / **external**) financing since these funds are generated by operations. Issuing stocks and bonds are forms of (**internal** / **external**) financing since these funds come from investors outside of the firm.

Q12   Review the financial information of this company and *comment* on
     a.   signs of financial strength.

     b.   warning signs or signs of financial weakness.

Q13   If you had $10,000, would you consider investing in this company?   (**Yes** / **No**)   Why or why not?

TEST YOUR UNDERSTANDING
Analyzing the Balance Sheet

Purpose: · Understand and interpret amounts reported on the balance sheet

BALANCE SHEETS		($ in millions)		
ASSETS	**CORP A** 3/31/2006	**CORP B** 2/28/2006	**CORP C** 3/31/2006	**CORP D** 3/31/2006
Cash and cash equivalents	$ 53.9	$1,472.1	$ 1,362.1	$ 382,766.0
Short-term investments	0.0	535.0	1,066.4	239,552.0
Accounts receivable	59.5	2,466.6	766.5	42,569.0
Inventories	42.1	2,034.2	0.0	0.0
Other current assets	79.4	536.8	171.9	0.0
Property, plant, and equipment	2,758.2	3,283.2	1,344.8	0.0
Accumulated depreciation	(1,008.6)	(1,684.8)	(569.8)	0.0
PPE, net	1,749.6	1,598.4	775.0	0.0
Goodwill	145.2	135.3	2,925.9	32,933.0
Long-term investments	0.0	0.0	3,189.9	789,772.0
Other non-current assets	44.7	739.8	567.7	98,609.0
TOTAL ASSETS	**$2,174.4**	**$9,518.2**	**$10,825.4**	**$1,586,201.0**
LIABILITIES				
Accounts payable	$ 523.0	$2,049.5	$ 985.7	$ 70,214.0
Short-term debt	2.2	254.7	0.0	337,670.0
Other current liabilities	0.0	0.0	323.7	628,157.0
Long-term debt	437.1	411.3	750.0	227,165.0
Other non-current liabilities	163.9	540.8	320.9	208,577.0
STOCKHOLDERS' EQUITY				
Contributed capital	404.7	1,420.5	6,624.1	18,174.0
Retained earnings	1,544.1	4,718.8	3,126.0	120,703.0
Other stockholders' equity	(900.6)	122.6	(1,305.0)	(24,459.0)
TOTAL L & SE	**$2,174.4**	**$9,518.2**	**$10,825.4**	**$1,586,201.0**

Classified Balance Sheets / Common-size Statements				($ in millions)			
	A 3/31/2006		**B** 2/28/2006		**C** 3/31/2006		**D** 3/31/2006
	Amount	CS%	Amount	CS%	Amount	CS%	Amount	CS%
Current assets	$ 234.9	10.8%	$7,044.7	74.0%	$ 3,366.9	31.1%	$ 664,887.0	41.9%
PPE, net	1,749.6	80.5%	1,598.4	16.8%	775.0	7.2%	0.0	0.0%
Other assets	189.9	8.7%	875.1	9.2%	6,683.5	61.7%	921,314.0	58.1%
TOTAL Assets	**$2,174.4**	**100.0%**	**$9,518.2**	**100.0%**	**$10,825.4**	**100.0%**	**$1,586,201.0**	**100.0%**
Current liabilities	$ 525.2	24.2%	$2,304.2	24.2%	$ 1,309.4	12.1%	$1,036,041.0	65.3%
LT liabilities	601.0	27.6%	952.1	10.0%	1,070.9	9.9%	435,742.0	27.5%
TOTAL Liab	**$1,126.2**	**51.8%**	**$3,256.3**	**34.2%**	**$ 2,380.3**	**22.0%**	**$1,471,783.0**	**92.8%**
Cont Capital	$ 404.7	18.6%	$1,420.5	14.9%	$ 6,624.1	61.2%	$ 18,174.0	1.1%
RE	1,544.1	71.0%	4,718.8	49.6%	3,126.0	28.9%	120,703.0	7.6%
Other SE	(900.6)	(41.4)%	122.6	1.3%	(1,305.0)	(12.1)%	(24,459.0)	(1.5)%
TOTAL SE	**$1,048.2**	**48.2%**	**$6,261.9**	**65.8%**	**$ 8,445.1**	**78.0%**	**$ 114,418.0**	**7.2%**

	CORP A 3/31/2006	**CORP B** 2/28/2006	**CORP C** 3/31/2006	**CORP D** 3/31/2006
RATIOS				
Current ratio	0.45	3.06	2.57	0.64
Debt ratio	0.52	0.34	0.22	0.93

Q1 Analyze the financial attributes of the four corporations on the previous page by placing an X in the box when the company has the characteristics noted below.

Which corporation …	CORP A	CORP B	CORP C	CORP D
Has significant cash and cash equivalents?				
Has significant receivables and inventory?				
Has no inventories?				
Has significant property, plant, and equipment?				
Has significant short-term and long-term investments?				
Finances assets primarily with… liabilities?				
contributed capital?				
retained earnings?				
Is the smallest company?				
Is the largest company?				

Q2 Use the descriptions below to match each corporation with their corresponding financial information. Then comment on why you selected the match.

BRINKER INTERNATIONAL (EAT) is the world's #2 casual-dining restaurant operator (behind Darden) with more than 1,500 restaurant locations in about 20 countries. Chili's Grill & Bar chain features southwestern-style dishes and has more than 1,100 restaurants, only trailing Applebee's as the largest full-service chain.
Brinker International must be Corporation ....(A / B / C / D).

Why?

CITIGROUP INC. (C) is one of the world's largest financial services firms, a leading credit card issuer, and the first United States bank with more than $1 trillion in assets. Citigroup offers banking, asset management, and investment banking through more than 3,000 locations in the United States and Canada and an additional 1,500 offices in 100 other countries. Subsidiaries include Salomon Smith Barney, CitiFinancial, and Primerica Financial Services. Citigroup is also a leader in online financial services.
Citigroup Inc. must be Corporation ....(A / B / C / D).

Why?

NIKE INC. (NKE) is the world's #1 shoe company with a 20% market share in the United States athletic shoe market. The company also sells a line of athletic apparel and equipment.
Nike Inc. must be Corporation..(A / B / C / D).

Why?

YAHOO! INC. (YHOO) is the leading Internet portal drawing more than 400 million visitors. Its site features a search engine and directory to help users navigate the Web with 20 international sites in 15 languages. Yahoo! compiles the news, financial information, online marketing, streaming media sources, and offers registered users personalized Web pages, e-mail, chat rooms, and message boards. Most sales come from advertising on the website.
Yahoo! Inc. must be Corporation..(A / B / C / D).

Why?

APPLE COMPUTER (AAPL) ($ in millions) INCOME STATEMENT		
Fiscal year ended (fye)…		**9/24/2005**
Sales revenue		$13,931
Cost of goods sold (COGS)		9,888
Gross profit		**4,043**
Selling, general, administrative expense (SGA)	$1,859	
Research and development expense (R&D)	534	
Depreciation and amortization expense	0	
Other operating expenses	0	
Total operating expenses		2,393
Income from operations		**1,650**
Interest expense	$ 0	
Investment income	165	
Gains and losses on the sale of assets	0	
Total other revenues and expenses		165
Income from continuing operations before income tax		**1,815**
Provision for income tax		480
Income from continuing operations		**1,335**
Nonrecurring items		0
Net income		**$ 1,335**

CHAPTER 3 – INCOME STATEMENT

Activity 19   **THE MULTI-STEP INCOME STATEMENT**

Purpose: ·   Identify the types of accounts presented on the income statement
              ·   Understand the organization of the multi-step income statement

When amounts are requested, refer to the income statement of Apple Computer on the previous page.

Revenues are gross amounts earned by selling products or providing services to customers while engaging in the company's primary business activity. **Expenses** are the costs incurred to produce revenues or provide services and are reported in the accounting period they benefit. **Cost of goods sold** is the wholesale cost of inventory sold to customers at retail. It is an operating expense.

Q1   The *revenues* earned from the sale of Power Macintosh computers, PowerBooks, iMacs, iPods, iBooks, iTunes, and other related products and services totaled (**$_____million / can't tell**) and the *cost of those products totaled* (**$_____million / can't tell**).

Operating expenses are those expenses directly related to a company's primary business activity, such as selling, general, and administrative (SGA) expenses; research and development (R&D); and depreciation and amortization. **Other revenues and expenses** refer to *other than operating* revenues and expenses (or nonoperating), which includes financing expenses, investment income, and gains and losses on the sale of assets other than inventory.

Q2   The income statement on the pervious page lists (**2 / 3 / 4**) *operating expense* accounts (other than COGS) that total $_____ million. (**COGS / Operating expenses**) is(are) greater (**by far / by a little bit**), which is (**expected / unexpected**) for a manufacturing firm.

Q3   *Other revenues and expenses* refer to *other* than (**operating / investing / financing**) revenues and expenses. *Interest expense* reflects the firm's cost of borrowing and is a(n) (**operating / investing / financing**) cost that is classified on the income statement as an (**operating / other**) expense. *Investment income* (**does / does not**) result from Apple Computer's primary business activity, and therefore, should be classified as (**operating / other**) revenues. When retailers and manufactures sell inventory [**revenue / a gain (loss)**] is reported and when they sell property, plant, and equipment [**revenue / a gain (loss)**] is reported. For Apple Computer, *other revenues and expenses* total $_____ million.

Provision for income tax is income tax expense based on the amount reported for *income from continuing operations before income tax*. **Nonrecurring items** refer to events that the company expects never to occur again, which include (**D**)iscontinued operations and (**E**)xtraordinary items.

Q4   Apple Computer's *average income tax rate* was _____%.

Q5   *Nonrecurring items* are items that occur (**once / twice / continuously**) within the life of a company. Identify each of the following as either a (**D**)iscontinued or (**E**)xtraordinary type of nonrecurring item.
         (**D / E / C**)   PepsiCo sells off Pizza Hut, Taco Bell, and KFC.
         (**D / E / C**)   Due to global warming the tundra melts in Barrow, Alaska, resulting in flooding an entire plant and closing it indefinitely.

Q6   The income statement reports the results of operations (**as of a certain date / over a period of time**).

Q7   Income statement accounts are listed in (**alphabetical order / order of relationship to the primary business activity / no particular order**). Therefore, (**operating revenues / nonrecurring items**) are reported at the top and (**operating revenues / nonrecurring items**) are reported at the bottom of the income statement.

Activity 20   **MULTI-STEP SUBTOTALS AND TOTALS**

Purpose: ·   Identify subtotals and totals on the multi-step income statement and how they are computed
                     ·   Understand the information presented by each multi-step subtotal and total

Gross profit is *operating revenue* (those revenues earned in the primary business activity) less *cost of goods sold* (COGS, the most significant operating expense for most retail and manufacturing firms). It is the first indication of profitability.

Income from operations is operating revenue less all operating expenses. It indicates how well a firm is managed.

Income from continuing operations before income tax indicates profitability from both operating and non-operating activities.

Income from continuing operations indicates profitability from operating and non-operating activities including the impact of the income tax.

Net income is all revenues and gains less all expenses and losses from operating, non-operating, and nonrecurring items. It is also referred to as earnings, the bottom line, or the profit (loss).

When amounts are requested, refer to the income statement of Apple Computer for the fiscal year ended on 9/24/2005 on pages 28 or 32.

Q1   *Net sales* minus (**operating expenses / other revenues and expenses / COGS**) equals *gross profit* that totals \$_____ million.

Q2   Gross profit minus (**provision for income tax / operating expenses (other than COGS) / other revenues and expenses**) equals *income from operations* that totals \$_____ million.

Q3   Income from operations plus or minus (**provision for income tax / operating expenses / other revenues and expenses**) equals *income from continuing operations before income tax* that totals \$_____ million.

Q4   Income from continuing operations before income tax minus (**provision for income tax / other revenues and expenses / COGS**) equals *income from continuing operations* that totals \$_____ million.

Q5   Income from continuing operations plus or minus (**provision for income tax / nonrecurring items / other revenues and expenses**) equals *net income* that totals \$_____ million.

Q6   Net income can either be distributed to stockholders as (**dividends / gross profit / retained earnings**) or be retained in the business as (**dividends / gross profit / retained earnings**).

Q7   On the multi-step income statement, (**3 / 4 / 5 / 6**) different subtotals and totals provide helpful information for decision-makers.

Q8   The best basis for comparing companies within the same industry is (**Income from operations / Income from continuing operations / Net income**).   Why?

Q9   In this accounting period BLOOMIN' FLOWERS, a florist shop, purchased flowers from a wholesaler costing $20,000 and sold them to customers for $30,000. Wages and other operating expenses total $4,000. Back in the year 2000, the company purchased land for $1,500 (that was never utilized) and sold during this accounting period for $6,000. Record amounts that result from these events.

Sales revenue	$_____
Cost of goods sold	$_____
Gross profit	$_____
Operating expenses	$_____
Income from operations	$_____
Other revenues and expenses	$_____
Income from continuing operations before income tax	$_____

Q10   What is the difference between revenues, gains, and net income?

A SERIES OF MULTI-STEP INCOME STATEMENTS

Purpose:
- Understand the relationship between the trend of revenue and the trends of other income statement accounts
- Interpret the meaning of increases and decreases in the various income statement accounts
- Identify the meaning of parentheses reported on the financial statements
- Develop strategies for analyzing the income statement

APPLE COMPUTER (AAPL) INCOME STATEMENT ($ in millions)				
Fiscal year ended (fye)…	9/24/2005	09/25/2004	09/27/2003	09/28/2002
Sales revenue	$13,931	$8,279	$6,207	$5,742
Cost of goods sold (COGS)	9,888	6,020	4,499	4,139
Gross profit	**4,043**	**2,259**	**1,708**	**1,603**
Selling, general, admin expense (SGA)	1,859	1,421	1,212	1,109
Research and development expense (R&D)	534	489	471	446
Depreciation/amortization expense	0	0	0	0
Other operating expenses	0	23	26	31
Total operating expenses	2,393	1,933	1,709	1,586
Income from operations	**1,650**	**326**	**(1)**	**17**
Interest expense	0	3	8	11
Nonoperating revenues and expenses	165	60	101	81
Total other revenues and expenses	165	57	93	70
Income from continuing operations before income tax	**1,815**	**383**	**92**	**87**
Provision for income tax	480	107	24	22
Income from continuing operations	**1,335**	**276**	**68**	**65**
Nonrecurring items	0	0	1	0
Net income	**$ 1,335**	**$ 276**	**$ 69**	**$ 65**

When amounts are requested, refer to the series of income statements of Apple Computer presented above.

Q1 From 9/28/2002 to 9/24/2005 *revenues* (**increased / decreased**), which indicates the company is (**staying competitive within its industry / successful at controlling costs / well managed**).

Q2 *Cost of goods sold* (COGS) is a(n) (**revenue / expense / asset / liability**) account that *totaled* what amount for the fiscal year ended on
9/24/2005? $_____ million   9/25/2004? $_____ million   9/27/2003? $_____ million

The *beginning* balance of COGS was what amount for the fiscal year ended on
9/24/2005? $_____ million   9/25/2004? $_____ million   9/27/2003? $_____ million

Q3 What is the greatest expense for this company? (**COGS / SGA expense / provision for income tax**). What typical costs might be included in this expense?

Q4 A nonrecurring item was reported during fye (**9/24/2005 / 9/25/2004 / 9/27/2003 / 9/28/2002**).

Q5   Let's compare some trends in the data...

a.   From 9/28/2002 to 9/24/2005, *sales revenue* (**decreased / about doubled / way more than tripled**).

b.   From 9/28/2002 to 9/24/2005, *COGS* (**decreased / about doubled / way more than tripled**). This amount of increase is (**expected / unexpected**). Why?

c.   From 9/28/2002 to 9/24/2005, *research and development expenses* (**decreased / about doubled / increased by less than 25%**). What does this indicate?

d.   From 9/28/2002 to 9/24/2005, *interest expense* (**decreased / about doubled / increased by less than 25%**). What event might result in this trend?

e.   From 9/28/2002 to 9/24/2005, *net income* (**decreased / about doubled / way more than tripled**), which is an extremely (**favorable / unfavorable**) trend, indicating the company is (**selling more merchandise / collecting amounts due from customers / increasingly earning more revenues and gains than incurring expenses and losses**).

Q6   When preparing financial statements, use the following rules for placing parentheses.
- Accounts that are *typically* added or that can either be added or subtracted to compute net income, use no parentheses when added and parentheses when subtracted.
- Accounts that are *typically* subtracted to compute net income use no parentheses when subtracted and parentheses when added.
- Parentheses indicate (**to subtract / to add / to do the opposite of typical**).
- A minus sign may be used instead of parentheses.

For example, COGS is typically (**added / subtracted**) to arrive at net income, and therefore, no parentheses indicate to (**add / subtract**) the amount.

Q7   Develop a strategy to evaluate the income statement. Which line of the income statement would you look at first? Second? Third?   *Explain* why.

ACCRUAL ACCOUNTING AND GAAP

Purpose: · Understand accrual accounting and how it differs from cash accounting
· Apply the Realization Concept and the Matching Concept

GAAP requires that companies use *accrual accounting* to report revenues and expenses, which means that companies must comply with the Realization Concept and the Matching Concept described below.

> **GAAP #2: The REALIZATION CONCEPT** governs revenue recognition. Revenues are recognized in the accounting period…
> 1) The earnings process is substantially complete, and
> 2) The amount to be collected is reasonably determinable.

Q1 On December 1, 20X1 RETAIL STORE sells a $1,500 computer. Customer Nancy pays $500 in cash and signs an installment agreement for the remaining $1,000 to be paid in 20X2, the following year. On the income statement of RETAIL STORE, how much revenue should be recognized
  a. in 20X1? $_____
  b. in 20X2? $_____

> **GAAP #3: The MATCHING CONCEPT** governs expense recognition. On the income statement, all costs (expenses) incurred should be reported in the same accounting period as the revenues they helped to generate. Therefore…
> 1) If there is an associated cause and effect, report the expense in the same period as the revenues it helped to generate. Examples include cost of goods sold and commissions.
> 2) If there is not an associated cause and effect relationship, then use a systematic and rational allocation method if you can. Examples include depreciation and amortization.
> 3) If no association can be found, then expense immediately. Examples include advertising, utility, and administrative expenses.

Q2 In this accounting period, CYCLES GALORE purchased 10 bicycles for $100 each at wholesale and sold 6 bicycles for $300 each to customers. On the income statement of CYCLES GALORE, how much will be reported for…
  a. sales revenue? $_____
  b. cost of goods sold? $_____
  c. gross profit? $_____
  d. The cost of the four unsold bicycles will remain part of (**inventory / COGS / retained earnings**) reported on the (**BS / IS / RE / CF**). What amount will be reported? $_____

Q3 Kiger Kayaking, a sporting goods retailer, began operations on August 1, 20X1 with the following transactions during the first month of operation. Compute August net income (using accrual-based accounting) and the August 31 cash balance.

Accrual	Cash		
$	$	Aug 1	Paid August office rent of $3,000.
$	$	Aug 5	Purchased and paid $35,000 for merchandise inventory.
$	$	Aug 16	Sold merchandise for $40,000 to customers at retail that cost $22,000 wholesale. Received cash from customers.
$	$	Aug 17	Received and paid a $1,500 advertising bill for August, September, and October.
$	$	Aug 30	Paid September office rent of $3,000.
XXXXXX	$	Aug 31	Cash balance
$	XXXXXX	Aug 31	August net income

ANALYSIS: RATIOS

Purpose:
· Understand the information provided by profitability ratios
· Understand that an increasing trend is preferred for profitability ratios
· Understand that the expected range of ratios varies by industry
· Understand that comparing a ratio to industry norms enhances meaning
· Understand that reviewing a number of ratios helps to provide an overall impression of profitability
· Understand that caution should be used when comparing EPS between companies

The ***three types of analysis*** are Ratio Analysis, Trend Analysis (horizontal analysis), and Common-Size Statement Analysis (vertical analysis). ***Analysis reveals relationships*** by comparing amounts to:
(a) other amounts for the same period (ratios and common-size statements),
(b) the same information from a prior period (trend analysis),
(c) competitor information, and industry norms.

RATIOS

Profitability Ratios measure the ability to generate profits; the overall performance of a firm. A higher ratio indicates greater profitability. *See Appendix B – Ratios for additional ratio explanations.*

The **Asset Turnover (Asset T/O)** ratio measures how efficiently assets are used to produce revenue. It is a measure of asset management efficiency and of profitability.

$$\textbf{Asset Turnover} = \frac{\textbf{Revenue}}{\textbf{Total assets}}$$

The **Return-On-Sales (ROS)** ratio measures the profitability of each dollar of revenue. It expresses net income as a % of revenue. This ratio is also referred to as the *Net Profit Margin*.

$$\textbf{ROS} = \frac{\textbf{Net income}}{\textbf{Revenue}}$$

The **Return-On-Assets (ROA)** ratio measures how efficiently assets are used to generate a return for creditors and shareholders. A high ROA ratio depends on managing asset investments to produce the greatest amount of revenue and controlling expenses to keep net income high. ROA is the most comprehensive measure of profitability since it takes into account both the profitability of each dollar of revenue (ROS) and sales volume (Asset T/O). ROS x Asset T/O = ROA

$$\textbf{ROA} = \frac{\textbf{Net income}}{\textbf{Total assets}}$$

The **Return-On-Equity (ROE)** ratio measures how efficiently amounts invested by common shareholders are used to generate profits.

$$\textbf{ROE} = \frac{\textbf{Net income}}{\textbf{Stockholders' equity}}$$

Gross Profit Margin (GP%) compares gross profit to revenue. It expresses gross profit as a % of revenue. Gross profit is the first measure of profitability.

$$\textbf{GP\%} = \frac{\textbf{Gross profit}}{\textbf{Revenue}}$$

Earnings Per Share (EPS) of common stock indicates the amount of net income earned for one share of the company's common stock outstanding.

$$\textbf{EPS} = \frac{\textbf{Net income - Preferred dividends}}{\textbf{Number of common shares outstanding}}$$

Q1   Use the information below to answer the following questions.

fye 2005 ($ in millions)	J.C. Penney Corp (JCP)	INTEL (INTC)
Revenue	$18,424	$ (X)
Expense	(A)	26,693
Net income	$ 524	$ 7,516
ROS	_____%	_____%

a.   Calculate the values for (A) and (X). Revenue for INTC is approximately (**2 times / 10 times**) greater than revenue for JCP while net income for INTC is more than (**2 times / 10 times**) greater than net income for JCP.

b.   Examine the relationship between Revenue and Net Income.
1.   (**JCP / INTC**) corporation is generating the most net income from each dollar of revenue.
2.   This relationship is measured by the (**ROS / ROA / ROE**) ratio.
3.   Calculate ROS and record in the space provided above.
4.   What information does the ROS ratio help to reveal about these two companies?

Q2   *Use the chart below to answer the following questions*. Stock symbols are shown in parentheses.

For the year 2005	Industry Average for Personal Computer Systems	Apple Computer (AAPL)	DELL (DELL)	Gateway (GTW)
Asset Turnover (Asset T/O)	1.99	1.32	2.32	2.20
Return On Sales (ROS)	6.7%	9.6%	6.6%	0.5%
Return On Assets (ROA)	13.3%	12.7%	15.3%	1.1%
Return On Equity (ROE)	37.0%	19.6%	62.9%	8.1%
Gross Profit Margin (GP%)	20.8%	36.9%	19.3%	13.6%
Earnings Per Share (EPS)	NA	$1.56	$1.37	$0.08

a.   For AAPL, profits were _____ cents of each revenue dollar while _____ cents of each revenue dollar were used to pay for the costs of running the business.

b.   Companies invest in assets to generate additional revenue. AAPL earned _____ cent(s) in profit for each dollar invested in assets. Is a company with a greater ROA ratio using assets more efficiently to generate profits than a company with a lower ROA ratio? (**Yes / No / Can't tell**)

c.   For the companies above in the Personal Computer Systems industry, ROE varies (**greatly / little**). During 2005 AAPL earned _____ cents in profits for each dollar invested by common shareholders.

d.   When ROA > ROE the corporation is borrowing from creditors at an average rate that is (**lower / higher**) than the rate earned by shareholders. This indicates the company is (**effectively / not effectively**) using financial leverage that contributes to a (**strong / weak**) financial position. In a company with a strong financial position (**ROS / ROE**) < ROA < (**ROS / ROE**).

e.   One measure of sales volume is the (**ROS / ROA / ROE / Asset T/O**) ratio. Wal-Mart makes profits by generating a large volume of sales on items with low profitability. Therefore, the Asset T/O ratio for Wal-Mart should be relatively (**low / high / can't tell**). ROS x Asset T/O = (**ROA / ROE / GP%**), which is generally considered the (**least / most**) comprehensive measure of profitability.

f. During 2005, it cost AAPL _____ cents of each revenue dollar to produce Power Macintosh computers, PowerBooks, iMacs, iPods, iBooks, iTunes, and other related products and services leaving _____ cents of each revenue dollar to cover all remaining operating expenses, nonoperating expenses, and profits. The Gross Profit Margin (GP%) is the (**first / second / last**) indication of profitability. The information for both the numerator and denominator of the GP% ratio come from the (**balance sheet / income statement / statement of cash flows**).

g. The earnings per share (EPS) ratios are (**less than $5 / more than $5**) per share and reflect (**only common / only preferred / both common and preferred**) earnings per share.
What two events would result in greater EPS for a corporation?

h. For each of the six profitability ratios listed above, a(n) (**increasing / decreasing**) trend is considered favorable. Circle the ratio that is the *weakest* among the 3 companies.

i. Meaning is added to a ratio by comparing that ratio to industry norms since success may vary by industry. Cross out each ratio that is weaker than the Industry Average for Personal Computer Systems.

j. Which company appears to be the weakest? (**AAPL / DELL / GTW**) Why?

k. Which company appears to be the strongest? (**AAPL / DELL / GTW**) Why?

Q3 Earnings per share (EPS) information is provided for Company ABC and Company XYZ. For each situation below, determine if the additional financial information makes Company ABC or Company XYZ appear to be the better investment.

Company ABC EPS = $0.50	Company XYZ EPS = $2.00
a. Net income $1,000,000 # of shares 2,000,000 Company (**ABC / XYZ / Can't tell**) appears to be the better investment. Why?	Net income $1,000,000 # of shares 500,000
b. Year 20X1 20X2 20X3 EPS $0.10 $0.20 $0.50 Company (**ABC / XYZ / Can't tell**) appears to be the better investment. Why?	Year 20X1 20X2 20X3 EPS $8 $4 $2
c. Current market price = $5/share Company (**ABC / XYZ / Can't tell**) appears to be the better investment. Why?	Current market price = $60/share

d. *Identify* two ways to enhance the meaning of a single earnings per share amount.

Note: The price/earnings (P/E) ratio (Market value per share / EPS) compares the market value of one share to the earnings of one share of common stock.

ANALYSIS: TREND

Purpose: · Prepare a trend analysis and understand the information provided

The **TREND ANALYSIS** compares amounts of a more recent year to a base year. The base year is the earliest year being studied. The analysis measures the percentage of change from the base year.

Q1 For Apple Computer, use the amounts listed below to complete the trend indexes for *Income from continuing operations before income tax* and the lines below. Divide each amount by the amount for the base year. Record the resulting *trend index* in the shaded area. Use fye 9/28/2002 as the base year.

APPLE COMPUTER (AAPL)							($ in millions)	
Fiscal year ended	**9/24/2005**		**9/25/2004**		**9/27/2003**		**9/28/2002**	
(fye)…	Amount	Trend Index	Amount	Trend Index	Amount	Trend Index	**BASE YEAR**	
Sales revenue	$13,931	243	$8,279	144	$6,207	108	$5,742	100
Cost of goods sold	9,888	239	6,020	145	4,499	109	4,139	100
Gross profit	**4,043**	**252**	**2,259**	**141**	**1,708**	**107**	**1,603**	**100**
Operating expenses	2,393	151	1,933	122	1,709	108	1,586	100
Income from operations	**1,650**	**9,706**	**326**	**1,918**	**NA**	**NA**	**17**	**100**
Other revenues (expenses)	165	236	57	81	93	133	70	100
Income from cont oper B4 income tax	**1,815**		**383**		**93**		**87**	
Provision for income tax	480		107		24		22	
Income from cont operations	**1,335**		**276**		**69**		**65**	
Nonrecurring items	0	NA	0	NA	1	NA	0	NA
Net income	**$1,335**		**$ 276**		**$ 70**		**$ 65**	

* Amounts with opposite signs cannot be accurately compared.

Refer to the series of income statements and the trend analysis above to answer the following questions.

Q2 Sales growth was 143% (243 – 100) from fye 9/28/2002 to fye 9/24/2005 with the greatest increase during fye (**9/24/05 / 9/25/04 / 9/27/03 / 9/28/2002**). When sales revenue increases, expenses would be expected to (**increase / stay the same / decrease**). It is favorable when sales revenue increases by 143% and expenses increase at a rate that is (**greater / less**) than 143%. If an expense account increases at a rate greater than sales revenue, this most likely indicates costs (**were kept under control / got out of control**).

Q3 From fye 9/28/2002 to fye 9/24/2005, which of the following expenses increased at a greater rate than sales revenue? (**COGS / Operating expenses / Provision for income tax**). For Apple Computer, the most important cost to keep under control is (**COGS / operating expenses / provision for income tax**). Overall, it appears that Apple Computer costs (**were kept under control / got out of control**). Why?

Q4 Total (**revenues / expenses**) increased at a greater rate from fye 9/28/2002 to fye 9/24/2005. How you can tell?

Q5   The annual sales revenue growth rate can be compared between companies.
         Assume less than 5% is low, 5-15% is moderate, and over 15% is high.
     The average annual sales revenue growth rate from fye 9/28/2002 to fye 9/24/2005 (3 years) is (**low /
     moderate / high**).

Q6   Compute the *gross profit margin* (Gross profit / Revenue) for fiscal years ended:

     9/24/2005 _____%;   9/25/2004 _____%;   9/27/2003 _____%;   9/28/2002 27.9%

     During this time period the *gross profit margin* (**increased / decreased**), which is a (**favorable /
     unfavorable**) trend.

Q7   Compute the *return-on-sales ratio* (Net income / Revenue) for fiscal years ended:

     9/24/2005 _____%;   9/25/2004 _____%;   9/27/2003 _____%;   9/28/2002 1.1%

     During this time period the *return-on-sales ratio* (**increased / decreased**), which is a (**favorable /
     unfavorable**) trend. What does this trend indicate?

Q8   Operationally, the best year was fye (**9/24/05 / 9/25/04 / 9/27/03**). Why? List as many items as you
     can to support your response.

Q9   Operationally, the worst year was fye (**9/24/05 / 9/25/04 / 9/27/03**). Why? List as many items as you
     can to support your response.

Q10 Review the trend indexes for *other revenues (expenses)*. For fye 9/27/200 the trend index of 133 is
     (**greater / less**) than 100 indicating the amount for that year is greater than the (**base year / previous
     year**) amount. For fye 9/25/2004 the trend index of 81 is (**greater / less**) than 100 indicating the amount
     for that year is less than the (**base year / previous year**) amount.

Q11 It is easier to analyze Apple Computer (**before / after**) preparing the trend analysis. Why?

ANALYSIS: COMMON-SIZE STATEMENTS

Purpose: · Prepare common-size statements and understand the information provided

The **COMMON-SIZE INCOME STATEMENT** compares all amounts to revenues. The analysis measures each item as a percentage of revenue.

Q1   For Gateway and Hewlett Packard companies listed below, complete the common-size statements by dividing each item on the income statement by sales revenue. Record the resulting common-size percentage in the shaded area provided.

($ in millions) Fiscal year ended (fye)…	Gateway (GTW) 12/31/2005		DELL (DELL) 2/3/2006		Hewlett Packard (HPQ) 10/31/2005	
	Amount	CS%	Amount	CS%	Amount	CS%
Sales revenue	$3,854	%	$55,908	100.0%	$86,696	%
Cost of goods sold (COGS)	3,532	%	45,958	82.2%	66,224	%
Gross profit	**322**	%	**9,950**	17.8%	**20,472**	%
Selling, genl, adm expense (SGA)	321	%	5,140	9.2%	13,293	%
Research and development (R&D)	0	%	463	0.8%	3,490	%
Income from operations	**1**	%	**4,347**	7.8%	**3,689**	%
Other revenues and expenses	5	%	227	0.4%	(146)	%
Income from cont oper B4 tax	**6**	%	**4,574**	8.2%	**3,543**	%
Provision for income tax	0	%	1,002	1.8%	1,145	%
Income from cont operations	**6**	%	**3,572**	6.4%	**2,398**	%
Nonrecurring items	0	%	0	0.0%	0	%
Net income	**$ 6**	%	**$3,572**	6.4%	**$2,398**	%

Refer to the series of income statements and the common-size analysis above to answer the following questions.

Q2   The greatest amount of *sales revenue* was reported by **(GTW / DELL / HPQ)**, but the greatest *net income* was reported by **(GTW / DELL / HPQ)**.

Q3   The company that reported the highest ratio for…
   a.   Gross profit margin   **(GTW / DELL / HPQ)**
   b.   Income from operations as a percentage of sales   **(GTW / DELL / HPQ)**
   c.   ROS   **(GTW / DELL / HPQ)**
   d.   A **(higher / lower)** profitability ratio is preferred.

Q4   The company that reported the greatest percentage of expense for…
   a.   COGS   **(GTW / DELL / HPQ)**, which is considered **(favorable / unfavorable)**. Why?

   b.   SGA   **(GTW / DELL / HPQ)**, which is considered **(favorable / unfavorable)**. Why?

   c.   R&D   **(GTW / DELL / HPQ)**, which is considered **(favorable / unfavorable)**. Why?

Q5   During 2005, **(GTW / DELL / HPQ)** remained the #1 direct-sale computer vendor.
   (*Hint: Refer to company descriptions in Appendix A – Featured Corporations*)

ANALYSIS of HEWLETT-PACKARD COMPANY

Purpose: · Understand and interpret amounts reported on the income statement

HEWLETT-PACKARD (HPQ) INCOME STATEMENTS	($ in millions)			
Fiscal years ended...	**10/31/2005**	**10/31/2004**	**10/31/2003**	**10/31/2002**
Sales revenue	$86,696	$79,905	$73,061	$56,588
Cost of goods sold (COGS)	66,440	60,811	53,858	41,793
Gross profit	**20,256**	**19,094**	**19,203**	**14,795**
Selling, general, and admin expense (SGA)	11,184	10,496	11,012	8,763
Research and development expense (R&D)	3,490	3,563	3,651	3,368
Depreciation and amortization expense	622	603	563	402
Other operating expenses	1,593	275	1,081	3,260
Total operating expenses	16,889	14,937	16,307	15,793
Income from operations	**3,367**	**4,157**	**2,896**	**(998)**
Interest income (expense)	(13)	4	(29)	(75)
Gains and losses	189	35	21	52
Total other revenues and expenses	176	39	(8)	(23)
Income from cont operations B4 inc tax	**3,543**	**4,196**	**2,888**	**(1,021)**
Provision for income tax	1,145	699	349	(118)
Income from continuing operations	**2,398**	**3,497**	**2,539**	**(903)**
Nonrecurring items / Minority interest	0	0	0	0
Net income	**$2,398**	**$3,497**	**$2,539**	**($903)**

Refer to the series of income statements presented above to answer the following questions.

Q1   Since 10/31/2002, sales growth was $_____ million, which is a _____ % change in sales revenue. The annual sales growth rate can be compared between companies.
     Assume less than 5% is low, 5-15% is moderate, and over 15% is a high
     The three-year average annual sales growth rate is considered (**low / moderate / high**).

Q2   Using 10/31/2002 as the base year, compute the trend index on 10/31/2005 for...
   a.   Sales revenue   _____ trend index
   b.   Cost of goods sold   _____ trend index
   c.   Total operating expenses   _____ trend index

   d.   From 10/31/2002 to 10/31/2005, *COGS* increased at a (**greater / lesser**) rate than sales revenue, which is considered (**favorable / unfavorable**) because it MOST likely indicates the company is (**borrowing more / selling long-term assets / not controlling costs**). As a result, the gross profit margin will (**increase / decrease**).

   e.   From 10/31/2002 to 10/31/2005, *total operating expenses* increased at a (**greater / lesser**) rate than sales revenue, which is considered (**favorable / unfavorable**) because it MOST likely indicates the company is (**paying back debt / purchasing assets / controlling operating costs**). As a result, ROS will (**increase / decrease**).

Q3   Compute ROS (Net income / Revenue) for fiscal years ended on:

   10/31/2005 _____%; 10/31/2004 _____% 10/31/2003 _____% 10/31/2002 _____%
   The strongest ratio was reported for fye (**10/31/05 / 10/31/04 / 10/31/03 / 10/31/02**).

Q4   Review all of the information presented above. If you had $10,000, would you consider investing in this company? (**Yes / No**) Why?

ANALYSIS of GATEWAY, INC.

Purpose: · Understand and interpret amounts reported on the income statement

GATEWAY (GTW) INCOME STATEMENTS ($ in millions)				
	2005	**2004**	**2003**	**2002**
Sales revenue	$3,854.1	$3,649.7	$3,402.4	$4,171.3
Cost of goods sold (COGS)	3,531.6	3,342.7	2,938.8	3,605.1
Gross profit	**322.5**	**307.0**	**463.6**	**566.2**
Selling, general, and admin expense (SGA)	363.6	909.2	974.1	994.4
Research and development expense (R&D)	0.0	0.0	0.0	0.0
Depreciation and amortization expense	0.0	0.0	0.0	0.0
Other operating expenses	(40.5)	0.0	0.0	83.0
Total operating expenses	323.1	909.2	974.1	1,077.4
Income from operations	**(0.6)**	**(602.2)**	**(510.5)**	**(511.2)**
Interest income (expense)	0.0	0.0	0.0	0.0
Gains and losses	6.8	20.5	19.3	35.5
Total other revenues and expenses	6.8	20.5	19.3	35.5
Income from cont operations B4 tax	**6.2**	**(581.7)**	**(491.2)**	**(475.7)**
Provision for income tax	0.0	(14.1)	23.6	(178.0)
Income from continuing operations	**6.2**	**(567.6)**	**(514.8)**	**(297.7)**
Nonrecurring items / Minority interest	0.0	0.0	0.0	0.0
Net income	**$ 6.2**	**$(567.6)**	**$(514.8)**	**$(297.7)**

Refer to the series of income statements presented above to answer the following questions.

Q1 Since 2002, *sales revenue* has (**increased / decreased**) by $_____ million, which is a _____% change in sales revenue. The greatest expense is (**COGS / SGA / R&D**) followed by (**COGS / SGA / R&D**). Gateway is a (**manufacturing / retail / service**) company so COGS is (**expected / not expected**) to be the largest expense.

Q2 Compute common-size percentages during 2002 and 2005 for…

Common-size %	2005	2002
Sales revenue	%	%
COGS	%	%
Gross profit	**%**	**%**
Total operating expenses	%	%
Income from operations	**%**	**%**

Q3 Gateway received an income tax refund for fiscal years ended in (**2005 / 2004 / 2003 / 2002**). How can you tell?

Q4 Review all of the information presented above. Gateway appears to report a (**strengthening / steady / weakening**) operating position. *Support* your response with at least two observations.

TEST YOUR UNDERSTANDING
Analyzing the Income Statement

Purpose: · Understand and interpret amounts reported on the income statement

($ in millions)	CORP A 2005		CORP B 2005		CORP C 2005	
	Amount	CS%	Amount	CS%	Amount	CS%
Sales revenue	$4,079.2	100.0%	$15,035.7	100.0%	$38,826.0	100.0%
Cost of goods sold (COGS)	2,939.5	72.1%	9,579.5	63.7%	15,777.0	40.6%
Gross profit		%		%		%
Selling, genl, adm expense (SGA)	959.7	23.5%	2,730.2	18.2%	5,688.0	14.6%
Research and development (R&D)	0.0	0.0%	0.0	0.0%	5,145.0	13.3%
Depreciation and amortization	0.0	0.0%	0.0	0.0%	126.0	0.3%
Other operating expenses	6.6	0.2%	105.0	0.7%	0.0	0.0%
Interest income (expense)	(14.3)	-0.4%	(434.6)	-2.9%	(19.0)	0.0%
Investment income	0.0	0.0%	2.4	0.0%	577.0	1.5%
Other revenues (expenses)	0.0	0.0%	2.7	0.0%	(38.0)	-0.1%
Provision for income tax	58.1	1.4%	850.4	5.7%	3,946.0	10.2%
Nonrecurring items	0.0	0.0%	498.1	3.3%	0.0	0.0%
Net income	$	%	$	%	$	%

Q1 Compute gross profit, gross profit margin, net income, and the return on sales ratio for each corporation. Record the amounts in the appropriate space above.

Q2 Analyze the financial attributes of the three corporations by circling the corporation with …
    a.   the lowest GP%.
    b.   significant R&D expense.
    c.   significant interest expense.
    d.   the lowest ROS.

Q3 Use the descriptions below to match each corporation with their corresponding financial information.

ANHEUSER-BUSCH (BUD) is the world's largest brewer and the largest beer producer in the United States with approximately half of the market share. It makes Budweiser, the nation's top-ranked beer, along with Bud Light, Michelob, and Busch. It is the largest recycler of aluminum cans in the world and one of the largest manufacturers of aluminum cans in the United States. It also operates amusement parks Busch Gardens and Sea World. Anheuser-Busch has a debt ratio of 80%. Anheuser Busch must be Corporation .... **(A / B / C)**.

Why?

INTEL CORPORATION (INTC) is the largest producer of semiconductors in the world currently possessing 80% of the market share. Intel's most notable products include its Pentium and Celeron microprocessors. Intel also makes flash memories and is #1 globally in this market. Dell is the company's largest customer.
Intel must be Corporation .... **(A / B / C)**.

Why?

BORDERS GROUP (BGP) operates in the highly competitive retail industry of selling books, music, and movies through its subsidiaries. Borders must be Corporation .... **(A / B / C)**.

Why?

STATEMENT OF CASH FLOWS

($ in millions) SOUTHWEST AIRLINES (LUV)	12/31/2005	
CASH FLOWS FROM OPERATING ACTIVITIES		
Net income (loss)	$ 548.0	
Depreciation and amortization	502.0	
Deferred income tax	257.0	
Operating (gains) losses	65.0	
(Increase) Decrease in receivables	(9)	
(Increase) Decrease in inventories	0.0	
(Increase) Decrease in other current assets	(59)	
(Decrease) Increase in payables	855.0	
(Decrease) Increase in other current liabilities	120.0	
Other non-cash items	(50)	
Net cash from operating activities (NCOA)		$2,229.0
CASH FLOWS FROM INVESTING ACTIVITIES		
Sale of property, plant, and equipment	$ 0.0	
Sale of investments	6.0	
Purchase of property, plant, and equipment	(1,216)	
Purchase of investments	0.0	
Other investing changes, net	0.0	
Net cash from investing activities (NCIA)		(1,210)
CASH FLOWS FROM FINANCING ACTIVITIES		
Issuance of debt	$ 300.0	
Issuance of capital stock	132.0	
Repayment of debt	(149)	
Repurchase of capital stock	(55)	
Payment of dividends	(14)	
Other financing charges, net	(1)	
Net cash from financing activities (NCFA)		213.0
Effect of exchange rate changes		0.0
Net change in cash and cash equivalent		1,232.0
Cash and cash equivalents at year start		1,048.0
Cash and cash equivalents at year end		$2,280.0

CHAPTER 4 – STATEMENT OF CASH FLOWS

Activity 29   **UNDERSTANDING THE STATEMENT OF CASH FLOWS**

Purpose: ·   Understand cash inflows and cash outflows
           ·   Identify operating, investing, and financing activities

The ongoing operation of any business depends on its ability to generate cash from operations. It is *cash* that an organization needs to pay employees, suppliers, creditors, and investors…*not profits*. Therefore, the real issue is cash. The statement of cash flows organizes cash inflows and cash outflows as operating activities, investing activities, and financing activities since…

MANAGEMENT uses accounting information to make decisions regarding

Financing   -->   Investing   -->   Operating   -->

FINANCING ACTIVITIES: Creditors lend and owners contribute $$$ to finance a company.

INVESTING ACTIVITIES: The $$$ obtained through financing is used to purchase revenue generating assets such as property, plant, and equipment (PPE) and investment securities.

OPERATING ACTIVITIES: PPE and other revenue-producing assets are used to manufacture goods, offer services, and generate dividends and interest that in turn result in $$$ profits.

FINANCING ACTIVITIES: $$$ Profits are reinvested to internally finance the company.

INVESTING ACTIVITIES: The $$$ obtained through financing is used to purchase revenue generating assets…and the cycle continues.

TRANSACTIONS REPORTED ON THE STATEMENT OF CASH FLOWS	
OPERATING ACTIVITIES (Direct Method)	
CASH INFLOWS Cash from customers Cash from interest and dividends Other operating cash receipts	CASH OUTFLOWS Cash paid to suppliers Cash paid to employees Interest paid Other operating cash payments
INVESTING ACTIVITIES	
CASH INFLOWS Sell property, plant, equipment Sell investment securities Receive loan repayments	CASH OUTFLOWS Purchase property, plant, equipment Purchase securities Make loans
FINANCING ACTIVITIES	
CASH INFLOWS Borrow cash from creditors and issue debt securities (bonds) Issue equity securities (capital stock)	CASH OUTFLOWS Repay amounts borrowed (debt principal) Repurchase equity shares (treasury stock) Pay cash dividends

Q1 On the statement of cash flows, a positive amount indicates a cash (**inflow / outflow**), while a negative amount indicates a cash (**inflow / outflow**). Note: On the statement of cash flows, cash *outflows* may be identified by enclosing the amount within parentheses or preceding the amount with a minus sign.

Q2 Identify the following transactions as Operating, Investing, or Financing activities.

(**O / I / F**)	a.	Receive cash from customers
(**O / I / F**)	b.	Issue common stock
(**O / I / F**)	c.	Purchase property, plant, and equipment
(**O / I / F**)	d.	Pay cash to suppliers for amount on invoice
(**O / I / F**)	e.	Declare and pay cash dividends to common shareholders
(**O / I / F**)	f.	Pay insurance premiums for the coming year
(**O / I / F**)	g.	Repay long-term debt

Q3 For an established company, the expected primary source of cash is (**operating / investing / financing**) activities. Why?

Q4 *Refer to the cash flow information displayed below to answer the following questions.*

Southwest Airlines STATEMENT OF CASH FLOWS ($ in millions)			
	2005	**2004**	**2003**
Net cash from *operating* activities	$2,229	$1,157	$1,336
Net cash from *investing* activities	(1,210)	(1,850)	(1,238)
Net cash from *financing* activities	213	133	(48)

a. The primary source of cash is (**operating / investing / financing**) activities, which is considered (**favorable / unfavorable / depends**). Why?

b. The purchase and sale of long-term assets are reported as (**operating / investing / financing**) activities. This company is (**purchasing / selling**) assets, which is considered (**favorable / unfavorable / depends**). Why?

c. Borrowing funds, issuing stock, and paying dividends are reported as (**operating / investing / financing**) activities.

1. For this firm, borrowing and repaying debt are the primary financing activities.
   During 2003, financing activities reported a net cash (**inflow / outflow**), indicating this company was (**borrowing / paying off**) debt.
   During 2004, financing activities reported a net cash (**inflow / outflow**), indicating this company was (**borrowing / paying off**) debt.

2. For financing activities, a net cash (**inflow / outflow / depends**) is preferred. Why?

OPERATING ACTIVITIES

Purpose: · Understand operating activities on the statement of cash flows

OPERATING ACTIVITIES (Direct Method)	
CASH INFLOWS	**CASH OUTFLOWS**
Cash from customers	Cash paid to suppliers
Cash from interest and dividends	Cash paid to employees
Other operating cash receipts	Interest paid
	Other operating cash payments

Q1   Operating activities include cash transactions that primarily affect (**current asset / long-term asset / current liability / long-term liability / stockholders' equity**) accounts.

(Circle *all* that apply)

Q2   For operating activities, a net cash (**inflow / outflow**) is preferred.

Q3   Identify the transactions that are recorded in the operating section of the statement of cash flows.

(**Operating / Not**)	a.	Receive cash from customers paying on account
(**Operating / Not**)	b.	Pay rent for the next accounting period
(**Operating / Not**)	c.	Purchase factory equipment
(**Operating / Not**)	d.	Receive the utility bill for this accounting period that will be paid next accounting period
(**Operating / Not**)	e.	Accrue wage expense in an adjusting journal entry at year end

Southwest Airlines (LUV) STATEMENT OF CASH FLOWS ($ in millions)			
Cash Flows from Operating Activities			
	2005	**2004**	**2003**
Net income (loss)	$ 548	$ 313	$ 442
Depreciation expense	502	467	417
(Increase) decrease in accounts receivable	(9)	(75)	43
(Increase) decrease in inventory	0	0	0
Increase (decrease)in accounts payable	855	231	129
Other operating changes, net	333	221	305
Net cash from operating activities (NCOA)	**$2,229**	**$1,157**	**$1,336**

Refer to the information immediately above to answer the following questions.

Q4   The (**direct / indirect**) method is used to report cash flows from operating activities.

Q5   LUV reports a (**strong / weak**) cash position for operating activities. Support your response with at least two observations.

Q6   LUV operates all (**Boeing / Airbus / Raytheon**) aircraft. Why?
(*Hint: Refer to company descriptions in Appendix A – Featured Corporations*)

DIRECT AND INDIRECT METHODS
For Operating Activities

Purpose: · Understand the direct and indirect method of reporting operating activities

The operating activity section of the statement of cash flows can be reported using the direct or the indirect method. The *direct method* reports sources and uses of cash during the accounting period. The *indirect method* reports net income followed by amounts adjusting accrual-based "Net Income" to cash-based "Net Cash from Operating Activities."

STATEMENT A	Adapted from COCA-COLA
Fiscal year ended ($ in millions)	
Cash received from customers	$ 20,457
Cash paid to suppliers	(6,160)
Cash paid for operating expenses	(8,050)
Other expenses paid	(1,842)
Net cash from operating activities	$ 4,459

STATEMENT B	Adapted from COCA-COLA
Fiscal year ended ($ in millions)	
Net income (loss)	$ 3,751
Depreciation expense	863
(Increase) decrease in accounts receivable	(37)
(Increase) decrease in inventory	(21)
Increase (decrease) in accounts payable	80
Increase (decrease) in accrued expenses	(177)
Net cash from operating activities	$ 4,459

Q1   The (**direct** / **indirect**) format of the operating section starts with (**sales** / **net income**). Statement A above reports net cash from operating activities using the (**direct** / **indirect**) method, while Statement B uses the (**direct** / **indirect**) method.

Q2   The direct and indirect methods report the (**same** / **different**) amount for net cash from operating activities. However, the (**direct** / **indirect**) method reveals new information, while the (**direct** / **indirect**) method simply conveys amounts already reported on the income statement and changes in balance sheet accounts. Therefore, most companies choose the (**direct** / **indirect**) method so no additional information is shared with (**shareholders** / **suppliers** / **competitors**). (*Circle all that apply*)

Q3   Refer to Statement B above. Net cash from operating activities is (**greater** / **less**) than net income. This difference is primarily due to the adjustment for (**depreciation expense** / **change in accounts receivable**). Since most companies report depreciation expense, most companies also report net cash from operating activities as (**greater** / **less**) than net income.

Q4   Is it possible to report a net loss on the income statement and still report a net cash inflow from operating activities? (**Yes** / **No**) *Explain* why.

DIRECT METHOD
For Operating Activities

Purpose: · Prepare the operating section of the statement of cash flows using the direct method

Adapted from COCA–COLA

Balance Sheet	JAN 1	Adjustments		DEC 31	CHANGE
		Dr.	Cr.		
Current assets					
Cash	1,934			399	
Accounts receivable	1,882	A 20,494	B	1,919	37
Inventory	1,055	D	C	1,076	
Other current assets	2,300	G	F	2,300	
Current liabilities					
Accounts payable	3679	E	D	3,759	
Accrued expenses	4750	I	H	4,573	

Income Statement	Accrual		Adjustments	Cash J
Sales	20,494	A	(37)	20,457
Cost of goods sold	(6,165)	C		
Operating expense	(8,050)	F		
Depreciation expense	(863)			
Other expenses	(1,665)	H		
Net income	3,751		708	4,459

Statement of Cash Flows		Cash J
Cash received from customers	B	
Cash paid to suppliers	E	
Cash paid for operating expenses	G	
Accrued expenses paid	I	
Net cash from operating activities		4,459

Refer to the information above to answer the following questions.

Q1 For this company, the change in cash totals $_____, which is the sum of net cash from (**operating / investing / financing**) activities. (*Circle all that apply*)

Q2 Amounts from the beginning and ending balance sheet and the income statement can be used to estimate amounts for the statement of cash flows. Preparation of the operating section includes analyzing the (**current asset / long-term asset / current liability / long-term liability / stockholders' equity**) accounts on the balance sheet. (*Circle all that apply*)

Q3 To prepare the operating section, start by analyzing the first current asset account after cash. Accounts receivable is increased by (**credit sales / cash received from customers**) and decreased by (**credit sales / cash received from customers**). Use the beginning and ending balances of accounts receivable and sales* (A) on the income statement to compute cash received from customers $_____ (B).** Enter this amount at the locations labeled (B) in the above forms, which includes a credit to accounts receivable on the balance sheet and as cash received from customers on the statement of cash flows under the column labeled Cash J.

* Assume all sales are credit sales.
** Beg A/R $1,882 + Sales $20,494 = $22,376 – Cash received from customers $_____ = End A/R $1,919

Q4   The next current asset account, inventory, is increased by (**purchases** / **cost of goods sold**) and decreased by (**purchases** / **cost of goods sold**). (**Purchases** / **Cost of goods sold**) is reported on the income statement as $_____ million. Using the beginning and ending balances of inventory and cost of goods sold (C) from the income statement, compute purchases $_____ million (D)*. Enter this amount at the locations labeled (D) on the forms on the previous page.

Purchases increases (**accounts receivable** / **inventory**) and (**accounts payable** / **accrued expenses**). Accounts payable is increased by (**purchases** / **cash paid to suppliers**) and decreased by (**purchases** / **cash paid to suppliers**). Using the beginning and ending balances of accounts payable and purchases (D), compute cash paid to suppliers $_____ million (E)**. Enter this amount as a debit to accounts payable on the balance sheet and on the (**income statement** / **statement of cash flows**).

To compute cash paid to suppliers, (**1** / **2** / **3**) balance sheet accounts need to be analyzed.

Q5   Complete the preparation of the statement of cash flows by analyzing the remaining current asset and current liability accounts and using the associated amounts from the income statement. Cash paid for operating expenses totals $_____ million (G) (related balance sheet account is other current assets). Accrued expenses paid totals $_____ million (I) (related balance sheet account is accrued expenses). The operating section of the statement of cash flows just completed uses the (**direct** / **indirect**) format.

Q6   a.   *Net income* reported on the income statement is primarily based on (**accrual** / **cash**) accounting, while *cash from operating activities* reported on the statement of cash flows is primarily based on (**accrual** / **cash**) accounting.

b.   *Net income* includes (**sales revenue earned** / **cash received from customers**), while *cash from operating activities* includes (**sales revenue earned** / **cash received from customers**).

c.   *Net income* includes (**cost of goods sold** / **cash paid to suppliers**), while *cash from operating activities* includes (**cost of goods sold** / **cash paid to suppliers**).

Q7   Decision makers compare "net income" to "net cash from operating activities." To make these two amounts more comparable, it is preferable to report the same accounts on both the income statement and the operating activity section of the statement of cash flows.

Which of the following accounts are used to compute net income?   (*Circle all that apply.*)
(**Interest revenue** / **Interest expense** / **Dividend revenue** / **Dividends paid**)

- *Interest revenue* (**is** / **is not**) reported on the income statement, therefore, *interest payments received* are reported as a(n) (**operating** / **investing** / **financing**) activity on the statement of cash flows.
- *Interest expense* (**is** / **is not**) reported on the income statement, therefore, *interest payments* are reported as a(n) (**operating** / **investing** / **financing**) activity on the statement of cash flows.
- *Dividend revenue* (**is** / **is not**) reported on the income statement, therefore, *dividend payments received* are reported as a(n) (**operating** / **investing** / **financing**) activity on the statement of cash flows.
- *Dividends paid* (**are** / **are not**) reported on the income statement, therefore, *dividends paid* are reported as a(n) (**operating** / **investing** / **financing**) activity on the statement of cash flows.

* Beg inventory $1,055 + Purchases $_____ = $7,241 – COGS $6,165 = End Inventory $1,076
** Beg A/P $_____ + Purchases $_____ = $_____ – Cash paid to suppliers $_____
      = End A/P $_____

INDIRECT METHOD
For Operating Activities

Purpose: · Prepare the operating section of the statement of cash flows using the indirect method

Use the information and forms in the previous activity, DIRECT METHOD, to complete this activity.

Q1 To begin preparation of this format, transfer the amounts from the Statement of Cash Flows *column* labeled Cash J to the Income Statement *column* labeled Cash J (in the previous activity). When complete, each *row* should contain the accrual-based amount reported on the income statement and the corresponding cash-basis amount reported on the statement of cash flows. The cash-basis amount is zero for (**operating expense / depreciation expense**).

In the Adjustments Column of the income statement, enter the difference between the accrual-based amounts and the cash-based amounts. The row for sales has been completed for you. The adjustment amount is zero for (**operating expense / depreciation expense**).

Q2 On the balance sheet, compute the difference between the beginning and ending balances of each current asset and current liability account and enter the result in the *column* titled Change (in the previous activity). The change in accounts receivable has been completed for you.

Q3 Complete the operating section below using the information from the previous activity.

Statement of Cash Flows (Indirect Method)	Amounts
Net income	$
Add depreciation expense	
(Increase) decrease in accounts receivable	
(Increase) decrease in inventory	
(Increase) decrease in other current assets	
Increase (decrease) in accounts payable	
Increase (decrease) in accrued expenses	
Net cash from operating activities (NCOA)	**$4,459**

Q4 Use the completed indirect method information above to answer the following questions.

a. The adjustment for *accounts receivable* is (**positive / negative**) because cash-based cash received from customers is (**less / more**) than accrual-based sales. (**Accrual- and cash-based accounting / Beginning and ending balance sheet amounts**) indicate the *direction* of the adjustment. With regard to the direction of the adjustments, increases in current asset accounts are treated (**the same as/ differently from**) increases in current liability accounts.

b. The adjustment for inventory is a (**positive / negative**) $_____, the adjustment for accounts payable is a (**positive / negative**) $_____, and nets to a (**positive / negative**) $_____, which is the adjustment from accrual-based (**sales / cost of goods sold**) to cash-based cash paid to suppliers.

Q5 When using the *indirect method* identify whether the following amounts are added (+), subtracted (-), or are (**Not**) an adjustment from net income to cash from operating activities.

(**+ / - / Not**)	a.	Revenues earned and received in cash
(**+ / - / Not**)	b.	Noncash revenues reported on the income statement
(**+ / - / Not**)	c.	Expenses incurred and paid in cash
(**+ / - / Not**)	d.	Noncash expenses reported on the income statement
(**+ / - / Not**)	e.	Depreciation expense
(**+ / - / Not**)	f.	Gain on the sale of equipment

INVESTING ACTIVITIES

Purpose: · Understand investing activities on the statement of cash flows

INVESTING ACTIVITIES	
CASH INFLOWS	CASH OUTFLOWS
Sell property, plant, equipment	Purchase property, plant, equipment
Sell investment securities	Purchase securities
Receive loan repayments	Make loans

Q1 Investing activities include cash transactions that primarily affect the purchasing and selling of (**current assets / long-term assets / current liabilities / long-term liabilities / stockholders' equity**).
(Circle *all* that apply)

Q2 Identify the transactions that are recorded in the investing section of the statement of cash flows.
(**Investing / Not**)   a.   Sell equipment at a loss
(**Investing / Not**)   b.   Pay rent for the next accounting period
(**Investing / Not**)   c.   Purchase factory equipment
(**Investing / Not**)   d.   Purchase 100 shares of Coca-Cola common stock with the intent of holding the security long term
(**Investing / Not**)   e.   Issue additional shares of your company's common stock

Q3 A net *cash inflow* results from (**purchasing / selling**) more property, plant, and equipment. If a company is selling income-producing assets, resulting future revenues will most likely be (**higher / lower**), which is considered (**favorable / unfavorable**). However, if the asset being sold is an unprofitable division, then it would be considered (**favorable / unfavorable**).

Q4 A net *cash inflow* results from (**purchasing / selling**) investment securities. If the reason for selling the investments is to take profits, this is considered (**favorable / unfavorable**). If the reason for selling the investments is to finance operations, this is considered (**favorable / unfavorable**). If a gain is realized on the sale of assets (**more / less / the same amount of**) cash will be received than if a loss is reported.

Southwest Airlines (LUV) STATEMENT OF CASH FLOWS ($ in millions) Cash Flows from Investing Activities			
	2005	**2004**	**2003**
Sale of property, plant, and equipment (PPE)	$ 0.0	$ 0.0	$ 0.0
Sale of investments	6.0	0.0	0.0
Purchase of property, plant, and equipment	(1,216)	(1,809)	(1,238)
Purchase of investments	0.0	0.0	0.0
Other investing changes, net	0.0	(41)	0.0
Net cash from investing activities (NCIA)	**($1,210)**	**($1,850)**	**($1,238)**

Q5 *Refer to the accounting information immediately above to answer the following questions.*
a.   In 2005 LUV had a net cash (**inflow / outflow**) from the sale/purchase of PPE, which indicates the company is (**purchasing / selling**) more PPE. This most likely indicates the business is (**expanding / down-sizing**). What PPE items is LUV most likely purchasing/selling?

b.   LUV reports a (**strong / weak**) cash position for investing activities. *Why?*

FINANCING ACTIVITIES

Purpose: · Understand financing activities on the statement of cash flows

FINANCING ACTIVITIES	
<u>CASH INFLOWS</u> Borrow cash from creditors and issue debt securities (bonds) Issue equity securities (capital stock)	<u>CASH OUTFLOWS</u> Repay amounts borrowed (debt principal) Repurchase equity shares (treasury stock) Pay cash dividends

Q1   Financing activities include cash transactions that primarily affect (**current asset / long-term asset / current liability / long-term liability / stockholders' equity**) accounts.

(Circle *all* that apply)

Q2   Identify the transactions that are recorded in the financing section of the statement of cash flows.
   (**Financing / Not**)   a.   Purchase your company's common stock currently outstanding
   (**Financing / Not**)   b.   Declare and pay a cash dividend
   (**Financing / Not**)   c.   Issue preferred stock
   (**Financing / Not**)   d.   Call a bond payable currently outstanding
   (**Financing / Not**)   e.   Record a 2-for-1 stock split

Southwest Airlines (LUV) STATEMENT OF CASH FLOWS ($ in millions) Cash Flows from Financing Activities			
	2005	**2004**	**2003**
Issuance of debt	$300	$520	$ 0
Issuance of capital stock	132	88	93
Repayment of debt	(149)	(207)	(130)
Repurchase of capital stock	(55)	(246)	0
Payment of dividends	(14)	(14)	(14)
Other financing changes, net	(1)	(8)	3
Net cash from financing activities (NCFA)	$213	$133	($48)

Refer to the accounting information immediately above to answer the following questions.
Q3   In 2005 LUV had a net cash (**inflow / outflow**) from debt transactions, which indicates the company is (**issuing / repaying**) debt and, in general, is relying (**more / less**) on debt financing. If the debt is issued to finance growth and expansion, it is considered (**favorable / unfavorable**). However, if the debt is issued because cash from operating activities is insufficient, it is considered (**favorable / unfavorable**). Issuing additional debt (**does / does not**) dilute earnings per share.

Q4   In 2005 LUV had a net cash (**inflow / outflow**) from capital stock transactions, which indicates the company is (**issuing / purchasing**) its own stock. The ability to attract equity investors is (**favorable / unfavorable**). A company's own stock that is bought back with the intent to reissue to shareholders in the future is referred to as (**common / preferred / treasury**) stock, which (**increases / decreases**) shares outstanding and results in (**higher / lower**) earnings per share for current shareholders. Therefore, buying back a company's own stock is regarded (**favorably / unfavorably**) by current shareholders.

Q5   LUV is paying (**steady / random**) dividends.

Q6   LUV's cash position for financing activities (**is / is not**) appealing to shareholders. *Why?*

OPERATING, INVESTING, OR FINANCING?

Purpose: · Identify operating, investing, and financing activities on the statement of cash flows
·   Understand the amount reported and whether the transaction results in an inflow or an outflow of cash

Kristin Incorporated is preparing a statement of cash flows using the *direct method*.
- Identify the following transactions as Operating, Investing, or Financing by circling **O**, **I**, or **F**.
- Record the **$ amount** to be reported on the statement of cash flows. Designate cash inflows as a positive amount and cash outflows as a negative amount within parentheses.

Q1   Sell $2,000 of inventory to customers for $5,000 cash.   (**O** / **I** / **F**) $_____

Q2   Sell equipment with a book value (carrying value) of $65,000 for $50,000 cash.   (**O** / **I** / **F**) $_____

Q3   Borrow $100,000 from a bank at an annual interest rate of 7%. The note is due in three years.   (**O** / **I** / **F**) $_____

Q4   Issue 1,000 shares of $100 par, 6%, preferred stock for $180 per share.   (**O** / **I** / **F**) $_____

Q5   Pay $6,000 of accounts payable.   (**O** / **I** / **F**) $_____

Q6   Sell an investment in the common stock of Microsoft for $12,000 in cash. The common stock was originally acquired for $5,000 and at the end of the previous accounting period the market value was $11,000.   (**O** / **I** / **F**) $_____

Q7   On January 1st, purchase equipment for $50,000 cash down and a $150,000 long-term note payable.   (**O** / **I** / **F**) $_____

ANALYSIS: RATIOS

Purpose: ·   Understand the information provided by cash flow ratios

Cash Flow Ratios measure the company's ability to generate cash.

Free Cash Flow reflects the amount of cash available for business activities after allowances for investing and financing activity requirements to maintain productive capacity at current levels. Adequate free cash flow allows for growth and financial flexibility

| Free Cash Flow | = | **Net cash from operating activities (NCOA) - Capital expenditures required to maintain productive capacity - Dividends paid** |

The **Cash-Flow-Adequacy** ratio evaluates whether cash flow from operating activities is sufficient to cover annual payment requirements. The above ratio is defined to evaluate whether net cash from operating activities is adequate to maintain productive capacity at current levels. It presents free cash flow information in a ratio format. This ratio (with modifications in the denominator) is used by credit-rating agencies to identify if there is adequate cash coverage of capital expenditures, dividends, debt, and other annual payments.

| Cash Flow Adequacy | = | **Net cash from operating activities (NCOA)** |
| | | **(Capital expenditures required to maintain productive capacity + Dividends paid)** |

The **Cash-Flow-Liquidity** ratio compares cash resources to current liabilities. This ratio uses cash and marketable securities (truly liquid current assets) and net cash from operating activities to evaluate whether adequate cash is generated from selling inventory and offering services. Even a profitable business will fail without sufficient cash. It is a cash-basis measure of short-term liquidity.

| Cash Flow Liquidity | = | **(Cash + Marketable securities + NCOA)** |
| | | **Current liabilities** |

The **Quality-Of-Income** ratio compares cash flows from operating activities to net income. A ratio higher than 1.0 indicates high-quality income because each dollar of net income is supported by one dollar or more of cash. It is cash (not accrual-based net income) that is needed to pay suppliers, employees, etc., to invest in income-producing assets, and to ensure long-term success.

| Quality of Income | = | **Net cash from operating activities (NCOA)** |
| | | **Net income** |

SOUTHWEST AIRLINES (LUV) RATIOS ($ in millions)				
	2005	**2004**	**2003**	**2002**
FREE CASH FLOW				
Net cash from operating activities (NCOA)	$ 2,229.0	$ 1,157.0	$1,336.0	$ 520.2
Capital expenditures	(1,216.0)	(1,809.0)	(1,238.0)	(603.1)
Dividends paid	(14.0)	(14.0)	(14.0)	(13.9)
NCOA - Capital exp - Dividends paid	**$ 999.0**	**($666.0)**	**$ 84.0**	**($ 96.8)**
CASH FLOW ADEQUACY				
Net cash from operating activities (NCOA)	2,229.0	1,157.0	1,336.0	520.2
Capital expenditures + Dividends paid	1,230.0	1,823.0	1,252.0	617.0
NCOA / (Capital exp + Dividends paid)	**1.8122**	**0.6347**	**1.0671**	**0.8431**
CASH FLOW LIQUIDITY RATIO				
Cash and cash equivalents	2,280.0	1,305.0	1,865.0	1,815.4
Marketable securities (MS)	0.0	0.0	0.0	0.0
Net cash from operating activities (NCOA)	2,229.0	1,157.0	1,336.0	520.2
Current liabilities	3,848.0	2,142.0	1,723.0	1,433.8
(Cash + MS + NCOA) / Current liabilities	**1.17**	**1.15**	**1.86**	**1.63**
QUALITY OF INCOME				
Net cash from operating activities (NCOA)	2,229.0	1,157.0	1,336.0	520.2
Net income	548.0	313.0	442.0	241.0
NCOA / Net income	**4.1**	**3.7**	**3.0**	**2.2**

Use the information above to answer the following questions.

Q1 FREE CASH FLOW   Southwest Airlines would have been able to take advantage of a $200,000 opportunity during (**2005 / 2004 / 2003 / 2002**).

Q2 CASH FLOW ADEQUACY   Southwest Airlines did *not* have adequate cash for capital expenditures and dividends during (**2005 / 2004 / 2003 / 2002**), as indicated by a cash flow adequacy ratio of (**less / more**) than 1.0.

Q3 CASH FLOW LIQUIDITY RATIO   Southwest Airlines had enough cash resources to cover current liability obligations during (**2005 / 2004 / 2003 / 2002**), as indicated by a cash flow liquidity ratio of (**less / more**) than 1.0.

Q4 QUALITY OF INCOME   Southwest Airlines' quality of income ratio steadily (**increased / decreased**), which is a (**favorable / unfavorable**) trend.

Q5 In 2005, Southwest Airlines appears to (**have / not have**) an adequate ability to generate cash. Support your response with at least two observations.

SOURCES AND USES OF CASH STATEMENT

Purpose: · Prepare a sources and uses of cash statement and understand the information provided

SOUTHWEST AIRLINES (LUV)	STATEMENTS OF CASH FLOW			($ in millions)	
	Source/Use	2005	2004	2003	2002
Net cash from operating act (NCOA)	(S / U)	$2,229.0	$1,157.0	$1,336.0	$ 520.2
Sale of property, plant, equipment	(S / U)	0.0	0.0	0.0	0.0
Sale of investments	(S / U)	6.0	0.0	0.0	0.0
Purchase of property, plant, and equipment	(S / U)	(1,216.0)	(1,809.0)	(1,238.0)	(603.1)
Purchase of investments	(S / U)	0.0	0.0	0.0	0.0
Other investing cash flow items	(S / U)	0.0	(41.0)	0.0	0.0
Net cash from investing activities (NCIA)		($1,210.0)	($1,850.0)	($1,238.0)	($603.1)
Issuance of debt	(S / U)	300.0	520.0	0.0	385.0
Issuance of capital stock	(S / U)	132.0	88.0	93.0	56.8
Repayment of debt	(S / U)	(149.0)	(207.0)	(130.0)	(539.5)
Repurchase of capital stock	(S / U)	(55.0)	(246.0)	0.0	0.0
Cash dividends paid	(S / U)	(14.0)	(14.0)	(14.0)	(13.9)
Other financing cash flow items	(S / U)	(1.0)	(8.0)	3.0	(270.0)
Net cash from financing activities (NCFA)		$ 213.0	$ 33.0	($ 48.0)	($381.6)
Net change in cash		$1,232.0	($ 560.0)	$ 50.0	($464.5)

Q1   In the *column* labeled Source/Use above, identify each line item as a (S)ource or a (U)se of cash by circling S, U, or both if it could be either.

Q2   For 2005, transfer the amounts from the above Statement of Cash Flows to the below statement of Sources and Uses of Cash.

SOUTHWEST AIRLINES (LUV)	SOURCES AND USES OF CASH		($ in millions)	
	2005	2004	2003	2002
Cash from operating activities	$	$1,157.0	$1,336.0	$520.2
Sale of property, plant, equipment		0.0	0.0	0.0
Sale of investments		0.0	0.0	0.0
Other investing cash flow items		0.0	0.0	0.0
Issuance of debt		520.0	0.0	385.0
Issuance of capital stock		88.0	93.0	56.8
Other financing cash flow items		0.0	3.0	0.0
TOTAL Sources of cash	$2,667.0	$1,765.0	$1,432.0	$962.0
Purchase of property, plant, and equipment	$	($1,809.0)	($1,238.0)	($603.1)
Purchase of investments		0.0	0.0	0.0
Other investing cash flow items		(41.0)	0.0	0.0
Repayment of debt		(207.0)	(130.0)	(539.5)
Repurchase of capital stock		(246.0)	0.0	0.0
Cash dividends paid		(14.0)	(14.0)	(13.9)
Other financing cash flow items		(8.0)		(270.0)
TOTAL Uses of cash	($1,435.0)	($2,325.0)	($1,382.0)	($1,426.5)
NET change in cash	$ 1,232.0	($ 560.0)	$ 50.0	($ 464.5)

ANALYSIS: TREND

Purpose: · Prepare a trend analysis using the sources and uses of cash schedule and understand the information provided

A **TREND ANALYSIS** compares amounts of a more recent year to a base year. The base year is the earliest year being studied. The analysis measures the percentage of change from the base year.

Q1 For Southwest Airlines, use the amounts listed below to compute the trend indexes for the uses of cash. Divide each amount by the amount for the base year. Record the resulting *trend index* in the shaded area. Use 2002 as the base year.

SOUTHWEST AIRLINES (LUV)		SOURCES AND USES OF CASH			($ in millions)		
	2005		**2004**		**2003**		**2002**
	Amount	Trend Index	Amount	Trend Index	Amount	Trend Index	BASE YEAR
Net cash from oper activities (NCOA)	$ 2,229	428	$ 1,157	222	$ 1,336	257	$ 520.2	100
Issuance of debt	300	78	520	135	0	0	385.0	100
Issuance of capital stock	132	232	88	155	93	164	56.8	100
TOTAL Sources	$ 2,661	277	$ 1,765	183	$ 1,429	149	$ 962.0	100
Purchase of PPE	($1,216)		($1,809)		($1,238)		($ 603.1)
Repayment of debt	(149)		(207)		(130)		(539.5)
Cash dividends paid	(14)		(14)		(14)		(13.9)
TOTAL Uses	($1,435)		($2,325)		($1,382)		($1,426.5)

* Amounts with opposite signs cannot be accurately compared and division by zero is not applicable, so only applicable accounts are listed above and will not necessarily sum to the total.

Refer to the series of Sources and Uses of Cash Statements and the trend analysis above to answer the following questions.

Q2 Total sources of cash grew 177% (277 – 100) from 2002 to 2005 while total uses of cash grew _____% during the same period. Sources of cash grew at a (**greater / lesser**) rate than uses of cash, which is (**favorable / unfavorable.**)

Q3 The greatest growth in sources of cash was in the (**cash from operating activities / issuance of debt / issuance of capital stock**) account, which grew _____% from 2002 to 2005. This is extremely (**favorable / unfavorable**) since this is an (**internal / external**) source of cash.

Q4 The annual rate of growth in net cash from operating activities can be compared among companies.
   Assume less than 5% is low, 5-15% is moderate, and over 15% is high.
   The average annual rate of growth from 2002 to 2005 is (**low / moderate / high**).

Q5 Investing activities consisted of (**purchasing / selling**) PPE, which grew _____% from 2002 to 2005, which indicates the company is (**expanding / down-sizing**). The issuance of debt (**increased / decreased**) and the repayment of debt (**increased / decreased**). Debt is an (**internal / external**) source of cash. Issuance of capital stock grew _____% from 2002 to 2005. Cash dividends paid increased by _____% from 2002 to 2005.

Q6 Review the information above. Southwest Airlines appears to (**have / not have**) the ability to generate cash flows in the future. Support your response with at least two valid observations.

Activity 40

ANALYSIS: COMMON-SIZE STATEMENTS

Purpose: · Prepare common-size statements using the sources and uses of cash statement and understand the information provided

The **COMMON-SIZE SOURCES AND USES OF CASH** compares all amounts to total sources of cash of that same year. The analysis measures each item as a percentage of total sources of cash.

Q1 For 2004, complete the common-size statements by dividing each item on the statement of Sources and Uses of Cash by the amount of total sources of cash and record your results in the area provided below. To complete this, use the Sources and Uses of Cash information presented in Activity 38. Review the common-size information below. Were there any significant fluctuations in the sources or uses of cash from 2002 to 2005? (**Yes / No**) *Comment* on your observations.

SOUTHWEST AIRLINES (LUV) COMMON-SIZE SOURCES AND USES OF CASH				
	2005	**2004**	**2003**	**2002**
Net cash from operating activities (NCOA)	83.58%	%	93.30%	54.07%
Sale of property, plant, equipment	0.00%	%	0.00%	0.00%
Sale of investments	0.22%	%	0.00%	0.00%
Other investing cash flow items	0.00%	%	0.00%	0.00%
Issuance of debt	11.25%	%	0.00%	40.02%
Issuance of capital stock	4.95%	%	6.49%	5.90%
Other financing cash flow items	0.00%	%	0.21%	0.00%
TOTAL Sources of cash	**100.00%**	**100.00%**	**100.00%**	**100.00%**
Purchase of PPE	(45.59)%	%	(86.45)%	(62.69)%
Purchase of investments	0.00%	%	0.00%	0.00%
Other investing cash flow items	0.00%	%	0.00%	0.00%
Repayment of debt	(5.59)%	%	(9.08)%	(56.08)%
Repurchase of capital stock	(2.06)%	%	0.00%	0.00%
Cash dividends paid	(0.52)%	%	(0.98)%	(1.44)%
Other financing cash flow items	(0.04)%	%	0.00%	(28.07)%
TOTAL Uses of cash	**(53.81)%**	**(131.73)%**	**(96.51)%**	**(148.28)%**
Net change in cash	**46.19%**	**(1.73)%**	**3.49%**	**(48.28)%**

Refer to the series of common-size sources and uses of cash statements above to answer the following questions.

Q2 The primary source of cash is (**net cash from operating activities / issuance of debt / issuance of capital stock**) and the primary use of cash is (**purchasing PPE / repayment of debt /repurchase of capital stock / paying cash dividends**).

Q3 There was a decrease in cash during (**2005 / 2004 / 2003 / 2002**). What was the primary cause of this decrease?

Q4 There was an increase in cash during (**2005 / 2004 / 2003 / 2002**). What was the primary reason for this increase?

Q5 Southwest Airlines appears to (**have / not have**) the capacity to generate cash. Support your response with at least two observations.

ANALYSIS of ANHEUSER-BUSCH

Purpose: · Understand and interpret amounts reported on the statement of cash flows

ANHEUSER-BUSCH (BUD) STATEMENT OF CASH FLOWS ($ in millions)				
	2005	**2004**	**2003**	**2002**
Net income (loss)	$1,839.2	$2,240.3	$2,075.9	$1,933.8
Depreciation/amortization expense	979.0	932.7	877.2	847.3
Deferred income tax	0.2	187.1	129.5	160.2
Operating (gains) losses	(303.4)	(238.5)	(144.3)	(317.0)
(Increase) Decrease in receivables	14.7	(26.7)	(39.0)	0.0
(Increase) Decrease in inventory	35.8	(102.8)	(23.9)	0.0
(Increase) Decrease in other current assets	6.9	(21.6)	(60.5)	0.0
(Decrease (Increase) in payables	54.7	101.1	107.1	0.0
(Decrease (Increase) in other current liabilities	(41.1)	10.7	(37.6)	0.0
Other non-cash items	141.8	(142.0)	86.5	140.9
Net cash from operating activities (NCOA)	**$2,727.8**	**$2,940.3**	**$2,970.9**	**$2,765.2**
Sale of property, plant, equipment	0.0	0.0	0.0	0.0
Sale of investments	0.0	0.0	0.0	0.0
Purchase of property, plant, and equipment	(1,136.7)	(1,817.5)	(1,149.9)	(853.7)
Purchase of investments	0.0	0.0	0.0	0.0
Other investing cash flow items	48.3	302.5	0.0	0.0
Net cash from investing activities (NCIA)	**($1,088.4)**	**($1,515.0)**	**($1,149.9)**	**($ 853.7)**
Issuance of debt	100.0	1,443.8	1,389.0	1,151.8
Issuance of capital stock	135.5	120.8	88.6	145.4
Repayment of debt	(456.0)	(510.6)	(652.1)	(505.9)
Repurchase of capital stock	(620.4)	(1,699.5)	(1,958.9)	(2,027.0)
Cash dividends paid	(800.8)	(742.8)	(685.4)	(649.5)
Net cash from financing activities (NCFA)	**($1,641.7)**	**($1,388.3)**	**($1,818.8)**	**($1,885.2)**
Net change in cash	**(2.3)**	**37.0**	**2.2**	**26.3**
+ Beginning cash and cash equivalents	228.1	191.1	188.9	162.6
= Ending cash and cash equivalents	$ 225.8	$ 228.1	$ 191.1	$ 188.9
Net cash from operating activities (NCOA)	2,727.8	2,940.3	2,970.9	2,765.2
Purchase of property, plant, and equipment	(1,136.7)	(1,817.5)	(1,149.9)	(853.7)
Cash dividends paid	(800.8)	(742.8)	(685.4)	(649.5)
Free cash flow	**$ 790.3**	**$ 380.0**	**$1,135.6**	**$1,262.0**

Q1 The primary source of cash is (**operating / investing / financing**) activities, which typically indicates a (**strong / weak**) cash position. The company is (**purchasing / selling**) more property, plant, and equipment, which typically indicates a(n) (**expanding / contracting**) business.

Q2 During (**2005 / 2004 / 2003 / 2002**), the company borrowed more debt than it repaid, which might indicate the assumption of (**more / less**) financial risk. This company is (**paying / not paying**) dividends. During (**2005 / 2004 / 2003 / 2002**), the company repurchased more of its own stock than it issued, which is generally considered (**favorable / unfavorable**) for shareholders. *Why?*

Q3 Free cash flow (**is / is not**) adequate to cover annual cash needs. Overall, Anheuser-Busch reports a (**strong / weak**) cash position. *Support* your response with at least two observations.

ANALYSIS of GATEWAY

Purpose: · Understand and interpret amounts reported on the statement of cash flows

GATEWAY (GTW) STATEMENT OF CASH FLOWS ($ in millions)				
	2005	**2004**	**2003**	**2002**
Net income (loss)	$ 6.2	($567.6)	($514.8)	($297.7)
Depreciation/amortization expense	38.8	112.2	164.0	159.5
Deferred income tax	0.0	0.0	6.0	257.2
Operating (gains) losses	37.7	184.7	86.5	80.6
(Increase) Decrease in receivables	(8.7)	(59.3)	(23.6)	11.0
(Increase) Decrease in inventory	(23.0)	63.5	(25.4)	31.5
(Increase) Decrease in other current assets	(205.8)	40.8	306.3	(77.0)
(Decrease (Increase) in payables	222.6	(94.7)	137.7	(59.9)
(Decrease (Increase) in other current liabilities	(92.5)	(113.8)	(64.0)	(128.0)
Other non-cash items	0.0	0.0	0.0	(1.9)
Net cash from operating activities (NCOA)	**($24.7)**	**($434.2)**	**$ 72.7**	**($ 24.7)**
Sale of property, plant, equipment	13.9	12.1	401.1	447.4
Sale of investments	189.9	586.2	0.0	0.0
Purchase of property, plant, and equipment	(45.0)	(75.9)	(73.0)	(78.5)
Purchase of investments	(40.4)	(95.6)	(530.3)	(614.0)
Other investing cash flow items	0.0	(22.4)	20.0	9.9
Net cash from investing activities (NCIA)	**$118.4**	**$404.4**	**($182.2)**	**($235.2)**
Issuance of debt	0.0	340.9	0.0	0.0
Issuance of capital stock	1.1	11.7	1.8	0.4
Repayment of debt	0.0	0.0	0.0	0.0
Repurchase of capital stock	0.0	(280.0)	0.0	0.0
Cash dividends paid	0.0	(8.9)	(8.8)	(5.9)
Net cash from financing activities (NCFA)	**$ 1.1**	**$ 63.7**	**($ 7.0)**	**($ 5.5)**
Net change in cash	**94.7**	**33.9**	**(116.5)**	**(265.4)**
+ Beginning cash and cash equivalents	383.0	349.1	465.6	731.0
= Ending cash and cash equivalents	$477.7	$383.0	$349.1	$465.6
Net cash from operating activities (NCOA)	(24.7)	(434.2)	72.7	(24.7)
Purchase of property, plant, and equipment	(45.0)	(75.9)	(73.0)	(78.5)
Cash dividends paid	0.0	(8.9)	(8.8)	(5.9)
Free cash flow	**($69.7)**	**($519.0)**	**($ 9.1)**	**($109.1)**

Q1   Review operating activities and *comment* on your observations.

Q2   Review investing activities and *comment* on your observations.

Q3   Review financing activities and *comment* on your observations.

Q4   Gateway reports a (**strengthening / weakening**) cash position.
      Support your response with at least two observations.

TEST YOUR UNDERSTANDING
Statement of Cash Flows

Purpose:　·　Understand and interpret amounts reported on the statement of cash flows

Q1　The primary source of cash for an established company with a strong cash position should be (**operating / investing / financing**) activities.

Q2　a.　OPERATING ACTIVITIES report cash transactions that typically affect
(**CA / LTA / CL / LTL / SE**) accounts. (*Circle all that apply*)

　　b.　INVESTING ACTIVITIES report cash transactions that typically affect
(**CA / LTA / CL / LTL / SE**) accounts. (*Circle all that apply*)

　　c.　FINANCING ACTIVITIES report cash transactions that typically affect
(**CA / LTA / CL / LTL / SE**) accounts. (*Circle all that apply*)

Key:　CA *current asset*;　LTA *long-term asset*;　CL *current liability*;　LTL *long-term liability*;　SE *stockholders' equity*.

Q3　a.　Of the following accounts, circle those that are used to compute net income:
(**interest revenue / interest expense / dividend revenue / dividends paid**).

　　b.　Decision makers compare "net income" to "net cash from operating activities." To make these two amounts more comparable, it is preferable to report the same account information on both the income statement and the operating activity section of the statement of cash flows.

　　　　1.　Because interest revenue, interest expense, and dividend revenue are reported on the income statement, the cash received/paid for these items is also reported on the statement of cash flows in the (**operating / investing / financing**) activity section.

　　　　2.　Because dividends paid are NOT reported on the income statement, they are also NOT reported on the statement of cash flows in the (**operating / investing / financing**) activity section. Instead, dividends paid are reported in the (**operating / investing / financing**) activity section of the statement of cash flows.

Q4　a.　For a note receivable, receiving repayment of principal is a(n) (**operating / investing / financing**) activity, while receiving an interest payment is a(n) (**operating / investing / financing**) activity.

　　b.　For a loan payment, paying the principal is a(n) (**operating / investing / financing**) activity, while paying the interest is a(n) (**operating / investing / financing**) activity.

　　c.　Issuing common stock to shareholders is a(n) (**operating / investing / financing**) activity, and paying cash dividends to those shareholders is a(n) (**operating / investing / financing**) activity.

Q5   *Answer the questions that follow by referring to the statement of cash flow information below.*

COMPANY ($ in millions)	OPERATING	INVESTING	FINANCING
Ford (F)	$ 22,764	$ (17,169)	$ (2,976)
Royal Caribbean Cruises (RCL)	634	(1,784)	1,700
United Airlines (UAL)	(160)	(1,969)	2,138

   a.   The company that appears to be borrowing money to finance operating activities is
         (Ford / Royal Caribbean / United Airlines).

   b.   The company that appears to be borrowing money to expand and grow is
         (Ford / Royal Caribbean / United Airlines).

   c.   The company that appears to be using amounts from operating activities to purchase property,
         plant, and equipment, repay debt, and pay dividends is
         (Ford / Royal Caribbean / United Airlines).

   d.   The company that appears to have the *weakest* cash position is
         (Ford / Royal Caribbean / United Airlines).

         Identify at least two observations that support your response.

Q6   a.   *List* three transactions that result in a *cash inflow* from investing activities.

          b.   *List* three transactions that result in a *cash outflow* from financing activities.

Q7   *Identify* what the statement of cash flows reveals about a company that the income statement does not.

Q8   Who can use the information on the statement of cash flows? For what purpose?

CHAPTER 5
INTERPRETING AND UNDERSTANDING
SPECIFIC ACCOUNTS

Activity 44   CASH AND CASH EQUIVALENTS

Purpose: ·   Reinforce understanding of cash and cash equivalents

ORACLE CORPORATION (ORCL)

($ in millions)	05/31/05	05/31/04	05/31/03
Cash and cash equivalents	$ 3,894	$ 4,138	$ 4,737
Short-term investments	908	4,449	1,782
Receivables	3,386	2,635	2,602
Prepaid expenses	291	114	106
Property, plant, equipment, net	1,142	1,068	1,062
Other long-term assets	10,266	359	775
TOTAL Assets	$20,687	$12,763	$11,064

NOTES TO CONSOLIDATED FINANCIAL STATEMENTS

Cash, Cash Equivalents, and Investments in Debt and Equity Securities.
Our investment portfolio consists of cash, cash equivalents, and investments in debt and equity securities. Cash and cash equivalents consist primarily of highly-liquid investments in time deposits of major banks, commercial paper, United States government agency discount notes, money market mutual funds, and other money market securities with original maturities of 90 days or less. Short-term investments primarily consist of commercial paper, corporate notes, and Unites States government agency notes with original maturities of greater than 91 days but less than one year.
    Source: Oracle Corporation Annual Report: Notes to the financial statements

Refer to the information presented above to answer the following questions:

Q1   For Oracle, highly-liquid investments with maturities of 90 days or less are classified as (**cash and cash equivalents** / short-term investments / long-term investments) and investments with maturities of greater than 91 days but less than one year are classified as (cash and cash equivalents / **short-term investments** / long-term investments). The definition of cash equivalents is reported (on the balance sheet / on the income statement / **in the notes to the financial statements**).

Q2   For Oracle, cash and cash equivalents plus short-term investments total $_____ million on 5/31/05 that is _____% of total assets, which seems like a (**high** / low) percentage.

Q3   One measure of cash flow adequacy is (**free cash flow** / the debt ratio / return on sales), which is the amount of cash available from operations after paying for planned investments in property, plant, and equipment and dividends.

Q4   Can a company ever have too much cash? (Yes / No)   Too little cash? (Yes / No)   Explain.

SHORT-TERM INVESTMENTS

Purpose: · Reinforce understanding of amounts reported for short-term investments

12/31/20X1 BALANCE SHEET ACCOUNTS

Cash	$ 30,000
Short-term investments -- Trading securities	200,000
Interest receivable	1,000
Total current assets	$231,000

20X1 INCOME STATEMENT ACCOUNTS

Unrealized loss on trading securities	$ 12,000
Interest revenue	4,000
Dividend revenue	5,000

Refer to the information presented above to answer the following questions. Assume this is the *first year* of operation.

Q1   Investments classified as short term are intended to be sold or liquidated in (**one year or less / more than one year**).

Q2   Trading securities are reported on the balance sheet at their (**acquisition cost / amortized cost / fair market value**). $_____ is the fair market value of the trading securities reported above. Since purchasing these trading securities, their market value has (**increased / decreased / can't tell**) by $_____. Since this is the first year of operation, these securities must have been originally purchased for $_____.

Q3   If these securities were sold next year, a(n) (**realized / unrealized**) loss would be reported if the selling price was less than the (**acquisition cost / fair market value at the end of last year / current fair market value**).

Q4   The amount of interest *earned* during this accounting period was $_____. Of this amount, $_____ was collected in cash during this accounting period and $_____ is the amount of cash to be received in the future.

Q5   The *other* in *other* revenues and expenses (also referred to as *other* gains and losses), refers to *other* than (**operating / investing / financing**).

Q6   The income statement accounts listed above would be reported on a multi-step income statement as (**operating expenses / other revenues and expenses**).

Q7   As a result of the financial statement information listed above, 20X1 net income will (**increase / decrease**) by $_____.

Activity 46   ACCOUNTS RECEIVABLE

Purpose: · Reinforce understanding of amounts reported on the financial statements for accounts
                  receivable
Purpose

12/31/20X5 BALANCE SHEET ACCOUNTS
Accounts receivable ....$ 90,000
Allowance for uncollectible accounts ....(4,000)
Accounts receivable, net 86,000

20X5 INCOME STATEMENT ACCOUNTS
Sales revenue $800,000
Uncollectible account expense... 15,000

Refer to the information presented above to answer the following questions:

Q1   The *allowance* for uncollectible accounts is the portion of (accounts receivable / net sales revenue) that
      is estimated as uncollectible and is reported on the balance sheet as a (current asset / long-term asset /
      current liability / long-term liability / stockholders' equity).

Q2   The total amount customers owe the company on account on 12/31/20X5 is $_____. Of this
      amount, $_____ is estimated to be uncollectible and $_____ is estimated to be collectible.
      As a result of the financial statement information listed above, total assets will increase by $_____.

Q3   Uncollectible-account *expense* is the portion of (accounts receivable / sales revenue) that is estimated
      as uncollectible and reported as (an operating expense / other revenues and expenses) on a multi-step
      income statement. Above, sales revenue earned during 20X5 totals $_____ and of that amount
      $_____ is estimated to be uncollectible.

Q4   Uncollectible-account expense is a(n) (estimated / known) amount calculated (at the end of / during)
      each accounting period and recorded as an adjustment. This is an application of the (cost / matching /
      reliability) principle. The adjustment to record uncollectible-account expense changes (total assets / net
      income / both / neither). *Explain* why.

Q5   Above, the (allowance / direct write-off) method is used to report uncollectible accounts. Using the
      above amounts, assume that $2,000 owed by Customer ABC was written off as uncollectible. After the
      write-off the accounts would report: Accounts receivable ($88,000 / $90,000 / $92,000), Allowance for
      uncollectible accounts ($2,000 / $4,000 / $6,000), and Accounts receivable, net ($84,000 / $86,000 /
      $88,000). The write-off of an uncollectible account changes (total assets / net income / both / neither).
      Explain why.

Note: Accounts receivable, net is also referred to as net realizable value.
        Uncollectible-account expense is also referred to as doubtful-account expense or bad-debt expense.
        Other revenues and expenses are also referred to as other gains and losses.

Activity 47   ETHICS AFFECTING FINANCIAL STATEMENT AMOUNTS
Accounts Receivable

Purpose: ·   Understand the effect ethical decisions have on amounts reported on the financial statements

A manager of a small electronics store would like to expand and also sell computers. The expansion would require seeking a loan from a local bank. The manager knows net income for this year is lower than what is needed to qualify for additional financing at his current bank. The manager also realizes some of the estimates used to calculate net income could be adjusted to make *net income* come within the qualifying range for an additional loan.

Q1   On the income statement, over-estimating uncollectible-account expense will result in

(understating / having no affect on / overstating) operating expenses.

(understating / having no affect on / overstating) net income.

Q2   On the balance sheet, over-estimating uncollectible-account expense will result in

(understating / having no affect on / overstating) the allowance for uncollectibles.

(understating / having no affect on / overstating) accounts receivable, net.

Q3   To qualify for the bank loan, the manager should (**over** / **under**) estimate uncollectible-account expense. *Explain* why.

Q4   Is intentionally misstating an estimate ethical? (**Yes** / **No** / **Maybe**) *Explain.*

Q5   Is intentionally misstating an estimate legal? (**Yes** / **No** / **Maybe**) *Explain.*

Q6   List some possible consequences if bank officials detect the misstatement of the estimate.

Q7   Discuss some ways the misstatement of uncollectible account expense could be detected by bank officials.

Q8   In general, unethical decisions make the (**short term** / **long term**) appear better, but may result in huge (**short-term** / **long-term**) costs.

INVENTORY

Purpose: ·   Reinforce understanding of amounts reported on the financial statements for inventory as a result of using the LIFO cost-flow assumption

GENERAL ELECTRIC COMPANY (GE)

Note 1: Summary of Significant Accounting Policies
Inventories. All inventories are stated at the lower of cost or realizable values. Cost for substantially all of GE's U.S. inventories is determined on a last-in, first-out (LIFO) basis. Cost of other GE inventories is primarily determined on a first-in, first-out (FIFO) basis.

Note 11: GE Inventories (Adapted)

December 31 ($ in millions)	20X2	20X1
Raw material and work in process	$ 4,894	$ 4,708
Finished goods	4,379	3,951
Unbilled shipments	372	312
	9,645	8,971
Less revaluation to LIFO	(606)	(676)
	$9,039	$8,295

Refer to Note 1 above to answer Q1 and Q2.

Q1   General Electric uses the (FIFO / Weighted Average / LIFO) inventory cost-flow assumption(s). *Hint:* Circle all that apply.

Q2   Does the answer for Q1 comply with the Consistency Principle? (Yes / No) *Explain.*

Refer to Note 11 above to answer Q3 through Q7.

Q3   On December 31, 20X2, the balance sheet would have reported inventories of ($9,645 / $9,039) million if the first-in, first-out (FIFO) method had been used to value all inventories and ($9,645 / $9,039) million if the last-in, first-out (LIFO) method were used to value the domestic portion of inventories.

Q4   Circle the effect the LIFO cost-flow assumption has had on reported financial statement amounts since GE began operations. As a result of using LIFO, GE has reported:
    a. $606 million (more / less) in ending inventory.
    b. $606 million (more / less) in cost of goods sold (COGS).
    c. $606 million (more / less) in income from continuing operations before tax.
    d.   assuming a 40% tax rate, $242 million ($606 million x 40%) (more / less) in tax expense.

Q5   The revaluation to LIFO (decreased / increased) from 20X1 to 20X2, which indicates there probably (was / was not) a LIFO liquidation.

Q6   In a period of inflation, the cost-flow assumption resulting in the lowest taxable income is (FIFO / Weighted Average / LIFO). This tax benefit is achieved by allocating the higher, more current inventory costs to (COGS / Ending Inventory).

Q7   General Electric would appear more profitable if it used (FIFO / LIFO) to determine the value of all inventories. Would it really be more profitable? (Yes / No) *Explain.*

ETHICS AFFECTING FINANCIAL STATEMENT AMOUNTS
Inventory

Purpose: ·   Understand the effect ethical decisions have on amounts reported on the financial statements

A manager of a men's clothing store receives a bonus based on the amount of *gross profit* earned by the department. This year the manager is only two thousand dollars short from qualifying for a sizable year-end bonus. The manager is in a position to have a portion of the inventory counted twice in the year-end physical inventory count. Cost of goods sold is adjusted for any changes to year-end inventory.

Q1   On the balance sheet, double counting a portion of ending inventory will result in

       (understating / having no affect on / overstating) ending inventory.

       (understating / having no affect on / overstating) total assets.

Q2   On the income statement, double counting a portion of ending inventory will result in

       (understating / having no affect on / overstating) cost of goods sold (COGS).

       (understating / having no affect on / overstating) gross profit.

Q3   To qualify for the year-end bonus, the manager (should / should not) double count over two thousand dollars of ending inventory. *Explain* why.

Q4   Is intentionally double counting ending inventory ethical? (Yes / No / Maybe) *Explain*.

Q5   Is intentionally double counting ending inventory legal? (Yes / No / Maybe) *Explain*.

Q6   List some possible consequences if upper management detects double counting of ending inventory.

Q7   Discuss some ways the double counting of inventory could be detected by management.

PROPERTY, PLANT, AND EQUIPMENT

Purpose: · Reinforce understanding of property, plant, and equipment amounts reported on the financial statements

12/31/20X5 BALANCE SHEET ACCOUNTS
Equipment $400,000
Accumulated depreciation .... (150,000)
Book value 250,000

20X5 INCOME STATEMENT ACCOUNTS
Depreciation expense $50,000
Gain on sale of equipment... 7,000
Loss on sale of land... 3,000

Refer to the financial statement information presented above to answer the following questions.

Q1   The amount originally paid (acquisition cost) to purchase the equipment was $_____, which was capitalized and recorded as a(n) (**long-term asset / expense**).

Q2   The portion of the equipment's original cost expensed since it was purchased is $_____. The cost allocated to 20X5 for use of the equipment is $_____. Assuming straight-line depreciation is used, it appears the equipment was purchased _____ years ago.

Q3   Depreciation expense is a(n) (**estimated / known**) amount recorded (**at the end of / during**) each accounting period as an adjustment, which is an application of the (**cost / matching / consistency**) principle. On a multi-step income statement, depreciation expense is reported as an (**operating expense / other gains and losses**).

Q4   The (**straight-line / double-declining-balance / neither**) method(s) of depreciation will result in greater depreciation the *first* year of an asset's useful life and the (**straight-line / double-declining-balance / neither**) method(s) will result in greater *total* depreciation over the asset's useful life.

Q5   Book value (**is / is not**) the same as current value. The primary purpose of depreciation is (**cost allocation / current valuation**). *Explain* what this means.

Q6   During the year, equipment was sold for $_____ more than (**acquisition cost / book value**) while land was sold for $_____ less than (**acquisition cost / book value**). The company got a better deal on the sale of the (**equipment / land / can't tell**). *Explain.*

Q7   As a result of the financial statement information above, $_____ will be added into total assets and 20X5 net income will (**increase / decrease**) by $_____.

Q8   By purchasing additional property, plant, and equipment, the company is investing in (**short-term / long-term**) income-producing assets that are expected to (**increase / decrease**) future revenues.

Activity 51   ETHICS AFFECTING FINANCIAL STATEMENT AMOUNTS
Property, Plant, and Equipment

Purpose: · Understand the effect ethical decisions have on amounts reported on the financial statements

Financial analysts have predicted that net income will increase by 5% for a major corporation. Corporate management has suggested that the controller do what is necessary to meet these predictions. The controller decides to examine depreciation expense since the amount is based on estimates of useful life and residual value and GAAP allows choices with regard to depreciation methods.

Q1   GAAP allows choices with regard to depreciation methods. In the first year of an asset's useful life, if the *straight-line* rather than the double-declining-balance depreciation method is used then:
    a.   reported depreciation expense will be (**lower** / **higher**), which leads to (**lower** / **higher**) net income.
    b.   reported accumulated depreciation will be (**lower** / **higher**), which leads to (**lower** / **higher**) book value and (**lower** / **higher**) total assets.

Q2   To make net income appear as favorable as possible, the controller should choose the (**straight-line** / **double-declining-balance**) depreciation method for assets placed in service during the current year.

Q3   Is intentionally choosing a depreciation method that reports higher net income ethical? (**Yes** / **No** / **Maybe**) Legal? (**Yes** / **No** / **Maybe**) *Explain.*

Q4   Depreciation expense is based on estimates of useful life and residual value. To make net income appear as *favorable* as possible, the controller should (**shorten** / **lengthen**) the useful life and (**raise** / **lower**) the residual value of the asset.

Q5   Is intentionally choosing an estimated useful life and residual value that report higher net income ethical? (**Yes** / **No** / **Maybe**) Legal? (**Yes** / **No** / **Maybe**) *Explain.*

Q6   a.   For financial statement purposes, a company generally prefers to report (**lower** / **higher**) net income, and therefore, would choose the (**straight-line** / **double-declining-balance**) depreciation method.
    b.   For income tax purposes, a company generally prefers to report (**lower** / **higher**) taxable income, and therefore, would choose the (**straight-line** / **double-declining-balance**) depreciation method.
    c.   Is intentionally choosing one depreciation method for financial statement purposes and a different method for income tax purposes ethical? (**Yes** / **No** / **Maybe**) Legal? (**Yes** / **No** / **Maybe**)

Q7   Identify at least three items that the controller can use to make net income appear more favorable with regard to the depreciation of assets placed in service during the current year that are both ethical and legal.

LONG-TERM INVESTMENTS

Purpose: · Reinforce understanding of investments classified as available-for-sale securities

Q1 Assume Winfield Corporation purchased 100 shares of Coca-Cola stock and 100 shares of IBM stock on 1/2/20X1. These equity securities are classified as available-for-sale because the intent is to hold them for several years. Refer to the related financial information below to answer the following questions.

	Fair Market Value			Cost
	12/31/20X3	12/31/20X2	12/31/20X1	1/2/20X1
COCA-COLA (100 shares)	$ 7,400	$ 5,300	$ 4,500	$ 4,600
IBM (100 shares)	11,400	7,600	6,000	10,000
Total	$18,800	$12,900	$10,500	$14,600

Q2 Complete the chart below to reflect how the above information would be reported on the financial statements.

BALANCE SHEET	12/31/20X3	12/31/20X2	12/31/20X1
ASSETS: Long-term investments	$	$	$
SE: Accumulated other comprehensive income -- *Unrealized gain/(loss) on investments*	$	$	$
INCOME STATEMENT	**20X3**	**20X2**	**20X1**
Other comprehensive income -- *Unrealized gain/(loss) on investments*	$	$	$
STATEMENT OF CASH FLOWS	**20X3**	**20X2**	**20X1**
INVESTING ACTIVITIES: Cash inflows (outflows)	$	$	$

Q3 When available-for-sale securities increase in value, this event will…
   a. (increase / decrease / have no effect on) total assets,
   b. (increase / decrease / have no effect on) net income,
   c. (increase / decrease / have no effect on) comprehensive income, and
   d. (increase / decrease / have no effect on) stockholders' equity.

Q4 Assume the 100 shares of Coca-Cola stock were sold for $76 per share during 20X4. As a result, the 20X4 income statement would report a (**realized / unrealized**) gain of $_____ as an (**operating / other**) revenue and the 20X4 statement of cash flows would report a cash (**inflow / outflow**) of $_____ in the (**operating / investing / financing**) activity section.

Q5 When available-for-sale securities are sold at a gain, this event will…
   a. (increase / decrease / have no effect on) total assets,
   b. (increase / decrease / have no effect on) net income,
   c. (increase / decrease / have no effect on) comprehensive income, and
   d. (increase / decrease / have no effect on) stockholders' equity.

CURRENT and LONG-TERM LIABILITIES

Purpose: · Reinforce understanding of amounts reported on the financial statements for current and long-term liabilities

<u>12/31/20X5 BALANCE SHEET ACCOUNTS</u>   (\$ in millions)

Accounts payable	\$6,245
Warranty liability	510
Income taxes payable	389
Current portion of long-term debt	271
Total current liabilities	7,415
Deferred income taxes	51
Post-retirement benefit liabilities	2,390
Bonds payable, 8%, mature in 2010	2,500
Bond discount	(156)
	2,344
Long-term debt	631

<u>20X5 INCOME STATEMENT ACCOUNTS</u>

Sales revenue	\$50,000
Post-retirement benefit expense	698
Warranty expense	275
Interest expense (related to the bond payable)	220

Refer to the information presented above to answer the following questions.

Q1   (**Current** / **Long-term**) liabilities are obligations due within one year or within the company's normal operating cycle if longer. Obligations due beyond that time are classified as (**current** / **long-term**) liabilities.

Q2   The purchase of inventory will usually increase the (**accounts** / **notes** / **mortgage**) payable account.

Q3   Warranty costs related to 20X5 sales total (**\$275** / **\$510** / **\$785**) million and warranty costs expected to be incurred in the future total (**\$275** / **\$510** / **\$785**) million. These amounts are (**known** / **estimated**).

Q4   There is (**\$271** / **\$631** / **\$902**) million of total debt outstanding (not including bonds). Of this amount, the company plans to pay (**\$271** / **\$631** / **\$902**) million during the following year and pay (**\$271** / **\$631** / **\$902**) million in later years.

Q5   When bonds payable are issued, they are recorded at their (**face** / **present**) value. After issuance, they are reported at their (**present** / **fair market** / **amortized**) value. The above bond has a current carrying value of \$_____ million that will continue to (**increase** / **decrease**) until maturity. At maturity, the issuing corporation will pay \$_____ million to the holder of the bond.

Q6   The bond payable was issued at a discount because the market interest rates were (**higher than** / **equal to** / **lower than**) 8%, and therefore, the actual cost of borrowing is (**greater than** / **equal to** / **less than**) 8%. This year's interest payment totaled (**\$156** / **\$200** / **\$220** / **\$250**) while this year's cost of borrowing totaled (**\$156** / **\$200** / **\$220** / **\$250**).

Q7   Post-retirement benefits are expensed and recorded as a liability in the year of (**employment** / **retirement**). This is an application of the (**matching** / **cost** / **reliability**) principle.

STOCKHOLDERS' EQUITY

Purpose: · Reinforce understanding of amounts reported on the financial statements for stockholders' equity

COCA-COLA COMPANY
December 31, 2005

Share-Owners' Equity	($ and shares in millions)
Common stock, $.25 par value	
Authorized: 5,600 shares	
Issued: 3,507 shares	$ 877
Capital surplus*.	5,492
Reinvested earnings	31,299
Accumulated other comprehensive income	(1,669)
Less treasury shares, at cost (1,138 shares)	19,644

* Assume capital surplus is all from issuing common stock above the par value.

Refer to the financial information above to answer the following questions.

Q1   The total amount of financing received from shareholders since incorporation is $_____ million and is generally referred to as _____. Common stock of the Coca-Cola Company was originally issued (**above / at / below / can't tell**) par at an average price of $_____ per share.

Q2   When additional shares of common stock are issued, this event will:
a.   (**increase / decrease / have no effect on**) total assets,
b.   (**increase / decrease / have no effect on**) net income,
c.   (**increase / decrease / have no effect on**) stockholders' equity, and
d.   (**increase / decrease / have no effect on**) earnings per share.

Q3   The amount of net income retained in the business and not yet distributed as dividends to the shareholders is $_____ million, which is generally referred to as _____.

Q4   Retained earnings (**is / is not**) a reservoir of cash available for dividends.

Q5   Treasury stock is considered (**issued / outstanding / retired**) but no longer (**issued / outstanding retired**). The average price paid for treasury stock is approximately $_____ per share.

Q6   When a company buys back its own stock, this event will:
a.   (**increase / decrease / have no effect on**) total assets,
b.   (**increase / decrease / have no effect on**) net income,
c.   (**increase / decrease / have no effect on**) stockholders' equity, and
d.   (**increase / decrease / have no effect on**) earnings per share.

Q7   The number of common shares currently *outstanding* is #_____ million shares, which represents 100% ownership of the company.

Q8   Total stockholders' equity is $_____ million, which is the amount of business assets owned by shareholders.

Q9   List several factors that would attract you to purchase shares of stock in a particular corporation.

CURRENT MARKET INTEREST RATES

Purpose: · Benchmark current market rates and understand why they differ among various financial instruments

Q1 Research the following current interest rates. These rates are available on the Internet and at a local bank or credit union.

The current rates banks/credit unions are offering/asking are

a. _____% for a regular savings accounts.

b. _____% for a one-year certificate of deposit (CD).

c. _____% for a 30-year fixed-rate mortgage with no points.

d. _____% for a standard credit card.

Please note the source of your information: _____
   (financial institution, newspaper, website, etc.)

Q2 The current prime-lending rate is _____%, which is the interest rate charged by banks to their most creditworthy customers (usually the most prominent and stable business customers).

Please note the source of your information: _____
   (financial institution, newspaper, website, etc.)

Q3 Explain why the reported interest rates differ between (a) and (b) above.

Q4 Explain why the reported interest rates differ between (b) and (c) above.

Q5 Explain why the reported interest rates differ between (c) and (d) above.

Q6 Explain the prime lending rate and its importance with regard to other lending rates.

EXAMINING BOND YIELDS

Purpose: · Understand why bond yields differ

YIELD COMPARISONS

CORPORATE BONDS

Maturity		Rating	Yield
1-10	years	High quality (AAA-AA)	2.95%
1-10	years	Medium quality (A-BBB/Baa)	3.92%
10+	years	High quality (AAA-AA)	5.34%
10+	years	Medium quality (A-BBB/Baa)	5.95%
all	years	High yield (BB/Ba-C)	9.23%

NEW TAX-EXEMPT BONDS

Maturity (rating)			Yield
7-12	years	G.O. (AA)	3.30%
12-22	years	G.O. (AA)	4.19%
22+	years	G.O. (AA)	4.70%

Refer to the information in the table above to answer the following questions.

Q1   Yield is the cost to the issuing entity for borrowing, and the return to the investor/creditor for lending the money. Yield is also referred to as the market rate and the effective rate of borrowing.

  Record the yield of a *high-quality* corporate bond that matures in *1-10 years*.   _____%

Q2   Ratings are a measure of risk. Standard and Poor's and Moody's are two companies that assess the amount of risk. A rating of AAA indicates very low risk and a rating of C indicates very high risk.

  a.   Record the yield of a *high-quality* corporate bond that matures in 1-10 years.   _____%
  b.   Record the yield of a *high-yield* corporate bond.   _____%
  c.   *Explain* why one yield is higher than the other for these two types of corporate bonds.

Q3   Bonds have different lengths of time to maturity.
  a.   Record the yield of a high-quality corporate bond that *matures in 1-10 years*.   _____%
  b.   Record the yield of a high-quality corporate bond that *matures in over 10 years*.   _____%
  c.   *Explain* why one yield is higher than the other for these two types of corporate bonds.

Q4   Bonds issued by corporations are usually not tax-exempt, while bonds issued by municipalities usually are tax-exempt.
  a.   Record the yield of a high-quality *corporate bond* that matures in 10+ years.   _____%
  b.   Record the yield of a high-quality *tax-exempt bond* that matures in 7-12 years.   _____%
  c.   *Explain* the advantage of tax-exempt bonds to the investor/creditor.

  d.   *Explain* why one yield is higher than the other for these two types of bonds.

EXAMINING THE BOND MARKET

Purpose: · Understand why bonds sell at a premium, at par, or at a discount

HIGH-YIELD BONDS

Name	Rating	Coupon Rate	Maturity	Bid Price	Yield*
Allied Waste	B+	10.00 %	8/2014	104.50	8.71%
Trump AC	CCC+	11.25 %	5/2011	79.00	21.13%

* Yield is the lower of yield to maturity and yield to call.

Refer to the information in the table above to answer the following questions.

Q1   The Allied Waste bond has a _____% coupon rate (also referred to as the stated rate or the face rate) that determines the (**cash interest payment / effective interest rate**). An investor/creditor holding a $100,000 Allied Waste bond will receive $_____ in interest payments each year.

Q2   The Allied Waste bond is currently rated a B+ and returning a _____% yield, while the Trump AC bond is rated _____ and returning a _____% yield.

The CCC+ rating indicates (**more / less**) financial risk than a B+ rating. Therefore, to attract investors/creditors the Trump AC bond must offer a (**higher / lower**) rate of return (yield).

Q3   An investor/creditor purchasing the Allied Waste bond is expecting an _____ % annual return. Assuming investments with the same amount of risk, an investor/creditor would prefer a (**high / low**) yield while the issuing corporation would prefer a (**high / low**) yield.

Q4   The amount paid by the issuing corporation at maturity is referred to as the face value, the par value, and the maturity value. Bond bid (selling) price is quoted as a percentage of par.

For example, the Bid Price of the Allied Waste bond is 104.50. This indicates an investor/creditor could purchase or sell a $100,000 Allied Waste bond for $104,500. ($100,000 x 104.50%). This bond is selling at a (**premium / par / discount**).

A $100,000 Trump AC bond would sell for $_____. This bond is selling at a (**premium / par / discount**).

Q5   The Allied Waste bond is selling at a premium because the coupon rate (stated rate, face rate) is (**greater than / less than**) the yield (market rate, effective rate) for this investment. To achieve the (**higher / lower**) yield, the investor/creditor pays the issuing corporation an additional amount (premium) at the beginning of the investment.

The Trump AC bond is selling at a discount because the coupon rate (stated rate, face rate) is (**greater than / less than**) the yield (market rate, effective rate) for this investment. To achieve the (**higher / lower**) yield, the initial investment of the investor/creditor is less than face value (discount) and at maturity the higher face value is received.

Q6   Would you prefer to invest in the Allied Waste or the Trump AC bond? Why?

Activity 58   EXAMINING THE DOW JONES INDUSTRIAL AVERAGE
Using the Internet

Purpose: · Understand how the DJIA is computed
            · Understand the information provided by the DJIA average

Q1   Companies comprising the Dow Jones Industrial Average (DJIA). The DJIA is the most quoted stock
      market index. On October 1, 1928 the first DJIA was computed using (10 / 20 / 30) industrial stocks
      traded on the New York Stock Exchange. Since then the corporations comprising the index have changed
      many times to reflect the changing economy. What stocks currently comprise the DJIA? Use the Internet
      to find out and list 6 of the 30 companies that currently comprise the DJIA.

      _____   _____   _____   _____   _____   _____

Q2   Computing the DJIA. The index started as a true average of the market values of the stocks comprising
      the index. In 1928, the sum of the market values of the each of the 30 stocks totaled $6,000 / 30 stocks =
      200 DJIA points. However, the average computation needed to be adjusted for stock splits and stock
      dividends. On October 3, 2005 the market values added together totaled $1,276.33 divided by a divisor
      of 0.12493117 = DJIA of 10,216 points.

      On October 3, 2005 if each of the 30 DJIA stocks increased in value by one dollar per share then the
      DJIA would increase by approximately 240 points (30/0.12493117 = 240). On October 3, 2005 assume
      the DJIA increased by approximately 500 points. This means that on average, each DJIA company
      would have increased in value by $_____ per share. When the DJIA increases in value, then the
      majority of stocks traded on the New York Stock Exchange would also be expected to (increase /
      decrease) in value.

Q3   Historical Summary of the DJIA. The following chart summarizes the DJIA at various points in
      history. Using the information presented in the chart, complete the graph outlined below.

      Date   DJIA
      1928 200
      1981 1,000
      1986 2,000
      1991 3,000
      1995 4,000
      1995 5,000
      1996 6,000
      1997 7,000
      1997 8,000
      1998 9,000
      1999 10,000
      1999 11,000

      Current information:

      _____   _____

	DJIA
13,000	
12,000	
11,000	
10,000	
9,000	
8,000	
7,000	
6,000	
5,000	
4,000	
3,000	
2,000	
1,000	

      1928 '38 '48 '58 '68   '81 '91 2001 2011

Q4   Use the Internet to find the current DJIA. DJIA closed at _____ points on _____ (date).
      Update the above chart and graph with the DJIA closing information just recorded.

Q5   Over the years the DJIA has had its ups and downs, but since 1928 the general direction of the DJIA has
      been (increasing / decreasing). What is the significance of the trend to investors? To the corporations
      issuing the stock?

FOLLOWING THE STOCK MARKET
Using the Internet

Purpose:
· Follow the stock market quotes for three companies and the Dow Jones Industrial Average (DJIA) for four weeks
· Understand market value per share

Q1 Select three publicly-traded corporations. For each of the next four weeks record in the chart below the (a) date of the stock information, (b) the closing stock price of the three companies you selected, and (c) the DJIA as of the close (end) of that business day.

Free stock quote information can be found on the Internet at moneycentral.msn.com; finance.yahoo.com; and other sites.

Corporation Name	Company #1	Company #2	Company #3	DJIA
WEEK ONE: Closing Market Price on _____ (a)				
WEEK TWO: Closing Market Price on _____				
WEEK THREE: Closing Market Price on _____				
WEEK FOUR: Closing Market Price on _____ (b)				
Four week change in market price (b) - (a)				
Four week % change in market price (b - a) / (a)	%	%	%	%

Q2 *At the end of the four weeks* complete the following:

a. Compute the information requested in the bottom two rows of the above chart.

b. Over the four weeks you observed the DJIA (**increased / stayed the same / decreased**).

c. Did the stocks you selected move in the same direction as the Dow Jones Industrial Average? (**Yes / No**)

d. Would you expect your stocks to move in the same direction as the DJIA? (**Yes / No**) *Explain* why.

e. *Comment* on at least two interesting results you noted while following the stock market.

CHAPTER 6 - COMPREHENSIVE REVIEW

Activity 60   TRANSACTIONS AFFECTING TOTAL ASSETS

Purpose: ·   Review the effect of various transactions on total assets

Circle whether each of the following events/transactions will (I)ncrease, (D)ecrease, or have (No) effect on *total assets*.

		TOTAL ASSETS *Circle the answer*
a.	Purchase equipment on account.	(I / D / No)
b.	Purchase supplies for cash.	(I / D / No)
c.	Record depreciation for the equipment.	(I / D / No)
d.	Sell equipment at a gain for cash.	(I / D / No)
e.	Record a cash sale to customer ABC.	(I / D / No)
f.	Record a sale on account to customer XYZ.	(I / D / No)
g.	Record the receipt of cash from customer XYZ in (f).	(I / D / No)
h.	Purchase short-term trading securities for cash.	(I / D / No)
i.	At the end of the accounting period, the short-term trading securities purchased in (h) have increased in market value.	(I / D / No)
j.	Land purchased ten years ago has increased in market value.	(I / D / No)
k.	The current market value of high-tech inventory is less than acquisition cost.	(I / D / No)
l.	Issue a bond payable at a discount for cash.	(I / D / No)
m.	Purchase treasury stock for cash.	(I / D / No)
n.	Pay cash dividends.	(I / D / No)

Activity 61   TRANSACTIONS AFFECTING TOTAL LIABILITIES

Purpose: · Review the effect of various transactions on total liabilities

Circle whether each of the following events/transactions will (I)ncrease, (D)ecrease, or have (No) effect on *total liabilities*.

TOTAL LIABILITIES
Circle the answer

a. Purchase inventory on account.   (I / D / No)

b. Pay for the inventory purchased in (a).   (I / D / No)

c. Hire a new employee for an annual salary of $20,000.
    The employee will start next Monday.   (I / D / No)

d. Issue bond payable at a discount.   (I / D / No)

e. Note payable is paid in full before the due date
    without penalty.   (I / D / No)

f. Retirement costs for current employees are recorded.
    These costs will not be paid until an employee retires
    in a future accounting period.   (I / D / No)

g. The end of the accounting period is on a Wednesday.
    Record accrued employee wage expense. Employees
    will get paid on Friday.   (I / D / No)

h. At the end of the accounting period,
    record accrued interest expense on a note payable.   (I / D / No)

i. At the end of the accounting period, estimate the
    amount of income taxes owed for the fiscal year.   (I / D / No)

j. Company ABC files a lawsuit. Company lawyers
    evaluate the case and estimate the company will
    probably win a substantial amount for damages.
    The case will be tried in a future accounting period.   (I / D / No)

k. A lawsuit is filed against Company ABC. Company
    lawyers evaluate the case and estimate the company will
    probably lose and owe a substantial amount for damages.
    The case will be tried in a future accounting period.   (I / D / No)

TRANSACTIONS AFFECTING TOTAL STOCKHOLDERS' EQUITY

Purpose: ·   Review the effect of various transactions on total stockholders' equity

Circle whether each of the following events/transactions will (I)ncrease, (D)ecrease, or have (No) effect on *total stockholders' equity*.

		TOTAL STOCKHOLDERS' EQUITY
		Circle the answer
a.	Issue preferred stock at par value.	(I / D / No)
b.	Purchase inventory on account.	(I / D / No)
c.	Issue bonds payable at a premium.	(I / D / No)
d.	Declare and issue a *cash* dividend.	(I / D / No)
e.	Declare and issue a *stock* dividend.	(I / D / No)
f.	Purchase treasury stock.	(I / D / No)
g.	During the accounting period, the market price of the corporation's common stock increases.	(I / D / No)
h.	Record net income for the accounting period.	(I / D / No)
i.	Correct an error that resulted in understating depreciation expense in the previous accounting period.	(I / D / No)

TRANSACTIONS AFFECTING NET INCOME

Purpose: · Review the effect of various transactions on net income

Circle whether each of the following events/transactions will (I)ncrease, (D)ecrease, or have (No) effect on *net income.*

		NET INCOME *Circle the answer*
a.	Record a sale for customer ABC paying cash.	(I / D / No)
b1.	Record a sale for customer DEF on account.	(I / D / No)
b2.	Record cash received from customer DEF for the sale recorded in (b1).	(I / D / No)
c1.	Purchase equipment.	(I / D / No)
c2.	At the end of the accounting period, make the adjusting entry to record depreciation for the equipment.	(I / D / No)
c3.	Record a loss on the sale of equipment.	(I / D / No)
d1.	Borrow $10,000 from the bank and sign a note.	(I / D / No)
d2.	At the end of the accounting period, make the adjusting entry to record accrued interest expense on the note in (d1).	(I / D / No)
d3.	Repay the $10,000 note.	(I / D / No)
e.	Pay rent for this accounting period.	(I / D / No)
f.	Record an extraordinary gain.	(I / D / No)
g.	Declare and issue a cash dividend.	(I / D / No)
h.	Issue common stock for more than the par value.	(I / D / No)
i.	At the end of the accounting period, record the portion of sales estimated as uncollectible.	(I / D / No)
j.	At the end of the accounting period, record an unrealized gain on the short-term trading securities portfolio.	(I / D / No)

Activity 64   # WHICH FINANCIAL STATEMENT?

Purpose: ·   Reinforce understanding of the information provided by each financial statement

Circle the financial statement you would consult to find the following information.
If more than one answer is correct, circle only one financial statement.

> BS   = Balance sheet
> IS   = Income statement
> RE   = Statement of retained earnings
> CF   = Statement of cash flows
> Not   = Not found on any of the financial statements

Circle only one correct answer

a.	Rental costs incurred this year.	(BS/IS/RE/CF/Not)
b.	Rental costs paid this year.	(BS/IS/RE/CF/Not)
c.	Rental costs still owed.	(BS/IS/RE/CF/Not)
d.	Cost of equipment allocated to this accounting period.	(BS/IS/RE/CF/Not)
e.	Equipment book value (carrying value).	(BS/IS/RE/CF/Not)
f.	Current market value of equipment purchased ten years ago.	(BS/IS/RE/CF/Not)
g.	Accrual-basis accounting used to compute operating results.	(BS/IS/RE/CF/Not)
h.	Cash-basis accounting used to compute operating results.	(BS/IS/RE/CF/Not)
i.	Noncash investing and financing activities.	(BS/IS/RE/CF/Not)
j.	Market value of investments in the short-term trading portfolio.	(BS/IS/RE/CF/Not)
k.	Unrealized gain on the available-for-sale investment portfolio.	(BS/IS/RE/CF/Not)
l.	Market value of the common stock issued by the corporation.	(BS/IS/RE/CF/Not)
m.	Amounts contributed by common shareholders.	(BS/IS/RE/CF/Not)
n.	Inventory remaining unsold at the end of the accounting period.	(BS/IS/RE/CF/Not)
o.	Inventory sold during the accounting period.	(BS/IS/RE/CF/Not)
p.	If we use the FIFO inventory cost flow assumption, the most current inventory costs will end up on this statement.	(BS/IS/RE/CF/Not)
q.	Evaluate how assets are currently being financed.	(BS/IS/RE/CF/Not)
r.	Financial statement reporting amounts as of a certain date.	(BS/IS/RE/CF/Not)

FINANCIAL STATEMENT PREPARATION

Purpose:
- Apply the revenue recognition and the matching principles
- Differentiate between accrual accounting and cash accounting
- Prepare a multi-step income statement, the statement of retained earnings, a classified balance sheet, and the operating activity section of the statement of cash flows

Betty opened Books Galore, Inc., for business on January 1, 20X1. The following financial items summarize the first year of operations. Use these items to prepare the 20X1 multi-step income statement, the 20X1 statement of retained earnings, the 12/31/20X1 classified balance sheet, and the operating activity section of the 20X1 statement of cash flows in the space provided.

a. Betty and her friend each invested $50,000 in cash (for a total of $100,000) in exchange for shares of common stock in Books Galore, Inc.

b. On January 1, 20X1, purchased new equipment costing $70,000 with a 10-year useful life and no residual value. Paid cash. Straight-line depreciation is used.

c. Rental costs for the year total $48,000. Of that amount, $4,000 remains unpaid on 12/31/20X1.

d. Purchased and paid $2,000 for a two-year property insurance policy.

e. On January 1, 20X1, purchased a piece of land next to the store for $20,000 in cash. Later in the year, the land was sold to another small business owner for $30,000 in cash.

f. During 20X1, customers purchased $300,000 of books. Of that amount, $250,000 has been collected from customers in cash and the remaining amounts will be collected next year.

g. Inventory purchases totaled $200,000 for the year. All purchases have been paid for, and $18,000 of those purchases remains in inventory at the end of the year.

h. On July 1, 20X1, borrowed $25,000 from a local bank and signed a one-year, 10% note payable. Principal and interest are due on June 30, 20X2.

i. The company paid shareholders cash dividends totaling $8,000.

j. At the end of the year, adjusting entries were recorded for depreciation expense and interest expense.

20X1 MULTI-STEP INCOME STATEMENT
For the Year Ended 12/31/20X1

Sales revenue
Cost of goods sold
Gross profit
Operating expenses:

Other revenues (expenses):

Net income

STATEMENT OF RETAINED EARNINGS
For the Year Ended 12/31/20X1

CLASSIFIED BALANCE SHEET
12/31/20X1

<u>Current Assets</u>

<u>Current Liabilities</u>

<u>Property, Plant, and Equipment</u>

<u>Stockholders' Equity</u>

STATEMENT OF CASH FLOWS
For the Year Ended 12/31/20X1
(Prepare using the direct method)

Cash flows from operating activities:
Receipts:

Payments:

Net cash from operating activities

Activity 66   RESEARCHING INDUSTRY NORMS

Purpose: ·   Introduce the concept of industry norms and how to research these statistics

Investors and creditors evaluate a corporation using many ratios that when reviewed together help to give an overall impression of corporate financial strength.

Meaning is added to a ratio by comparing that ratio to industry norms since ratios indicating success may vary by industry. A good example of industry differences is illustrated by the inventory turnover ratio. The rate at which a grocery store is expected to sell items of inventory is much quicker than a department store. This makes sense since a grocery store carries perishable goods that spoil if not sold fairly quickly, while a department store carries nonperishable items.

Meaning is also added to a ratio by comparing that ratio to ratios of previous years. Trends can then be evaluated as either favorable or unfavorable.

RESEARCHING INDUSTRY NORMS
Step one: Obtain the industry classification code for the company
There are two widely used industry classification systems: the Standard Industrial Classification (SIC) system and the North American Industry Classification System (NAICS). NAICS was developed in 1997 to replace the SIC system; however, many financial institutions and governmental agencies, including the Securities and Exchange Commission (SEC), continue to use the SIC system. Therefore, this text will use the SIC system.

The Standard Industrial Classification code is a coding system used to report information on U.S. businesses. It divides corporations into 10 major groups that are further divided into major categories. The first two digits refer to the Major Group code and describe the general nature of the activity. The final two digits refer to the specific activity. For example, the primary SIC code for General Motors is 3711. The 37 refers to the major group code for transportation equipment, and the 11 specifically to motor vehicles and car bodies. Many corporations engage in more than one type of business. The primary SIC code refers to the type of business with the greatest amount of revenue. The secondary SIC codes are listed in descending order according to revenue.

Step two: Research the industry average information using the SIC code or by the NAICS.
Printed references for industry average information include *Almanac of Business and Industrial Financial Ratios*, by Leo Troy, published by Prentice Hall, *Industry Norms and Key Business Ratios*, Dun and Bradstreet, Inc., *Standard and Poor's Industry Surveys, and Mergent's Industry Review*.
Free online references include *finance.yahoo.com, moneycentral.msn.com, www.hoovers.com, and www.sec.gov*.

Refer to the above information to answer the following questions.

Q1   To get an overall impression of corporate financial strength, investors and creditors should evaluate **(many ratios / only one or two ratios)**.

Q2   Industry norms for many ratios **(are the same / vary)** between industries.

Q3   A trend analysis of a ratio **(adds meaning to / confuses)** the evaluation.

Q4   Industry average information is reported by the four-digit _____ code.

Q5   The primary SIC code refers to the portion of the business with the greatest **(revenue / assets / market valuation)**.

RATIO ANALYSIS

Purpose:
- Understand that reviewing many ratios helps give an overall impression of corporate financial strength
- Understand that meaning is added to a ratio by comparing that ratio to industry norms or to a company within the same industry since norms may vary by industry

Industry Norm SIC 5651	RATIOS	THE GAP INC. (GPS)	American Eagle Outfitters (AEOS)
	LIQUIDITY		
NA	Working capital	$3,297.00	$719.10
2.30	Current ratio	2.50	3.60
1.00	Quick ratio	1.30	2.70
NA	Cash flow liquidity ratio	1.85	1.65
	LONG-TERM SOLVENCY		
0.14	Debt ratio	0.09	0.00
0.16	Debt-to-equity ratio	0.10	0.00
27.10	Times-interest-earned	53.10	NA
NA	Free cash flow	$772.00	$342.00
NA	Cash flow adequacy	1.99	3.77
	MANAGEMENT EFFICIENCY		
62.40	Accounts receivable turnover	NA	82.00
4.20	Inventory turnover	4.90	7.30
1.80	Asset turnover (Asset T/O)	1.70	1.60
NA	Accounts payable turnover	8.42	9.47
5.77	Accounts receivable days	NA	_____ days
85.71	Inventory days	73.47	_____ days
NA	Accounts payable days	42.76	_____ days
NA	Net trade cycle	30.71	_____ days
	PROFITABILITY		
40.00%	Gross profit margin	40.30%	46.50%
6.30%	Return-on-sales (ROS)	6.70%	12.70%
11.34%	Return-on-assets (ROA)	11.39%	20.32%
19.70%	Return-on-equity (ROE)	20.20%	24.80%
$1.20	Earnings per share	$1.20	$1.96
NA	Quality of income	1.39	1.58
	INVESTMENT		
17.5	Price/Earnings ratio (P/E)	14.10	16.80
NA	Dividend yield	1.90%	1.40%
NA	Dividend rate	$0.32	$0.45
$7.36	Book value per share	$6.33	$8.17
	Market value per share:		
NA	Close June 29, 2006	$17.44	$34.18
NA	52-week high	$22.19	$34.82
NA	52-week low	$15.90	$19.45

Refer to the ratio information on the previous page to answer the following questions.
For ratio formulas and explanations refer to Appendix B – Ratios.

Q1 For American Eagle, compute the following...
_____ account receivable days, _____ inventory days, _____ accounts payable days, and _____ days in the net trade cycle. Enter these amounts in the appropriate location in the ratio chart on the previous page. (GPS / AEOS) *net trade cycle* requires the least amount of working capital.

Q2 Break ROE into its components using the DuPont Analysis of ROE (found in Appendix B) for both The GAP and American Eagle. Use the ROE, ROS, and Asset Turnover ratio information from the previous page. Compute Financial Leverage.

GPS ROE = _____% = ROS _____% x Asset T/O _____ times x Financial Leverage _____
AEOS ROE = _____% = ROS _____% x Asset T/O _____ times x Financial Leverage _____

For each of the four above ratios, *circle* the stronger ratio. Between The GAP and American Eagle, the most significant difference in profitability can be attributed to (**ROS / Asset Turnover / Financial Leverage**), which indicates whether (**expenses / assets**) were effectively managed.

Q3 Compare The GAP Inc. and American Eagle Outfitters by *circling* the stronger ratio on the previous page. Compare The GAP to the industry norm by placing *a box* around the stronger ratio.

Q4 *Review the information for The GAP on the previous page for each category of ratio information and answer the questions below.* Support your responses with at least two significant observations.

a. LIQUIDITY RATIOS measure a firm's ability to meet cash needs as they arise. Does The GAP have the ability to meet cash needs as they arise? (**Yes / No**) *How can you tell?*

b. LONG-TERM SOLVENCY RATIOS measure the extent of debt relative to equity, if financial leverage is being used effectively, and the ability to cover interest, investing activity, financing activity, and other fixed payment requirements. Is The GAP effectively managing its debt? (**Yes / No**) Able to adequately cover capital expenditure costs and pay dividends? (**Yes / No**) *How can you tell?*

c. MANAGEMENT EFFICIENCY RATIOS measure the efficiency of managing cash, accounts receivable, inventory, PPE, and accounts payable. Is The GAP efficiently managing its assets? (**Yes / No**) *How can you tell?*

d. PROFITABILITY RATIOS measure the overall performance of a firm. Is The GAP providing a sufficient return to shareholders? (**Yes / No**) *How can you tell?*

e. INVESTMENT RATIOS compare the market value per share to other per share amounts and indicate the level of dividend payment. Based on the information presented on the previous page, would you recommend buying The GAP Inc. common stock? (**Yes / No**) *Why?*

TEST YOUR UNDERSTANDING
Comprehensive Analysis

Purpose:
- Analyze the income statement, the balance sheet, and the statement of cash flows
- Prepare a statement of retained earnings

CARNIVAL CORPORATION (CCL) BALANCE SHEET ($ in millions)				
ASSETS	11/30/2005	11/30/2004	11/30/2003	11/30/2002
Cash and cash equivalents	$ 1,178	$ 643	$ 610	$ 667
Short-term investments	9	17	461	39
Accounts receivable	408	409	403	108
Inventories	250	240	171	91
Other current assets	370	419	487	227
TOTAL Current assets	**2,215**	**1,728**	**2,132**	**1,132**
Property, plant, and equipment	25,331	24,184	20,073	12,103
Accumulated depreciation	(4,019)	(3,361)	(2,551)	(1,987)
PPE, net	**21,312**	**20,823**	**17,522**	**10,116**
Goodwill	4,488	4,627	4,355	681
Long-term investments	0	0	0	0
Other non-current assets	417	458	482	406
TOTAL Other	**4,905**	**5,085**	**4,837**	**1,087**
TOTAL ASSETS	**$28,432**	**$27,636**	**$24,491**	**$12,335**
Accounts payable	$ 690	$ 631	$ 634	$ 269
Short-term debt	583	981	94	0
Current portion of long-term debt	1,042	681	392	155
Accrued expenses	832	721	568	290
Other current liabilities	2,045	2,020	1,622	906
TOTAL Current liabilities	**5,192**	**5,034**	**3,310**	**1,620**
Long-term debt	5,727	6,291	6,918	3,014
Deferred income taxes	0	0	0	0
Other non-current liabilities	541	551	470	283
TOTAL Long-term liabilities	**6,268**	**6,842**	**7,388**	**3,297**
TOTAL Liabilities	**11,460**	**11,876**	**10,698**	**4,917**
Preferred stock	0	0	0	0
Common stock, par	359	359	355	6
Additional paid-in capital	7,381	7,311	7,163	1,089
Retained earnings	10,233	8,623	7,191	6,326
Other stockholders' equity	143	525	142	(3)
Treasury stock	(1,144)	(1,058)	(1,058)	0
TOTAL Stockholders' equity	**16,972**	**15,760**	**13,793**	**7,418**
TOTAL L & SE	**$28,432**	**$27,636**	**$24,491**	**$12,335**

CARNIVAL CORPORATION (CCL)	INCOME STATEMENT	($ in millions)		
Fiscal year ended...	11/30/2005	11/30/2004	11/30/2003	11/30/2002
Revenue	$10,735	$9,427	$6,459	$4,244
Cost of goods sold	4,822	4,244	2,880	1,764
Gross profit	5,913	5,183	3,579	2,480
SGA exp	2,474	2,288	1,680	1,067
Depreciation/amortization expense	902	812	585	382
Other operating expenses (revenues)	(102)	(90)	(69)	(11)
Operating expenses (other than COGS)	3,274	3,010	2,196	1,438
Income from operations	2,639	2,173	1,383	1,042
Interest income (expense)	(330)	(284)	(195)	(111)
Other revenues (expenses)	21	12	35	28
Income from continuing oper B4 inc tax	2,330	1,901	1,223	959
Provision for income taxes	73	47	29	(57)
Net income	$2,257	$1,854	$1,194	$1,016
Outstanding shares (in millions)	806	802	718	587

CARNIVAL CORPORATION (CCL)	STATEMENT OF CASH FLOWS	($ in millions)		
Fiscal year ended...	11/30/2005	11/30/2004	11/30/2003	11/30/2002
Net income (loss)	$2,257	$1,854	$1,194	$1,016
Depreciation/amortization expense	902	812	585	382
Operating (gains) losses	45	28	22	54
Changes in working capital	206	522	132	17
Net cash from operating activities (NCOA)	$3,410	$3,216	$1,933	$1,469
Sale of property, plant, equipment	0	0	0	0
Sale of investments	0	0	0	0
Purchase of property, plant, and equipment	(1,977)	(3,586)	(2,516)	(1,986)
Purchase of investments	0	0	0	0
Other investing cash flow items	7	497	83	(75)
Net cash from investing activities (NCIA)	($1,970)	($3,089)	($2,433)	($2,061)
Issuance of debt	910	881	1,751	232
Issuance of capital stock	50	112	42	7
Repayment of debt	(912)	(736)	(898)	(190)
Repurchase of capital stock	(305)	0	0	0
Cash dividends paid	(566)	(400)	(292)	(246)
Other financing cash flow items	(69)	64	223	(1)
Net cash from financing activities (NCFA)	($ 892)	($ 79)	$ 826	($ 198)
Effect of exchange rate changes	(13)	(15)	(23)	(5)
Net change in cash	535	33	303	(795)
+ Beginning cash and cash equivalents	643	610	667	1,421
= Ending cash and cash equivalents	$1,178	$ 643	$ 610	$ 667
Cash interest paid	$ 314	$ 250	$ 156	$ 110
Cash taxes paid	$ 15	$ 8	$ 20	$ 0
Free cash flow	$ 867	($ 770)	($ 875)	($ 763)

Refer to the financial statements presented for Carnival Corporation on the previous two pages to answer the following questions.

BALANCE SHEET

Q1　(1) Examine the following accounts, subtotals, and totals; (2) describe your observations; and then (3) identify what your observations indicate. A response is given for PPE, net to help with understanding.

　　a.　Property, plant, and equipment, net … *increased from $10,116 million to $21,312 million from 11/31/2002 to 11/31/2005, an increase of 111%, indicating purchases of additional cruise ships for expansion. The greatest increase was in fye 2003, when PPE almost doubled.*

　　b.　Goodwill …

　　c.　Long-term debt …

　　d.　Contributed capital totaled $_____ million on 11/31/2005 …

　　e.　Retained earnings...

Q2　Compute the ratios in the chart below. *For ratio formulas and explanation refer to Appendix B – Ratios.*

CARNIVAL CORPORATION	*Industry Norm*	11/30/2005	11/30/2003
Current ratio (CA / CL)	*0.50*		
Quick ratio (Cash + ST Invest+ AR / CL)	*0.40*		
Debt ratio (Total liabilities / Total assets)	*0.63*		
Times Interest Earned (Inc from oper / Int exp)	*8.00*		

　　For each ratio, (a) compare the two years of company ratios and circle the stronger ratio, (b) place a box around any company ratio that is stronger than the industry norm, and (c) c*omment* on the results.

Q3　The balance sheet indicates a (**strengthening / steady / weakening**) financial position. Why? *Comment* on your observations.

INCOME STATEMENT

Q4　Revenues were $_____ million for the earliest year reported and $_____ million for the most recent year reported. Since the earliest year reported, this account has changed by $_____ million, which is a _____% (**increase / decrease**). During the same time period, COGS (**increased / decreased**) by _____%, operating expenses (other than COGS) (**increased / decreased**) by _____%, and net income (**increased / decreased**) by _____%.

Q5   Compute the ratios in the chart below. *For ratio formulas and explanation refer to Appendix B – Ratios.*

CARNIVAL CORPORATION	Industry Norm	Fye 11/30/2005	Fye 11/30/2003
Gross profit margin (Gross profit / Revenue)	50.8%		
ROS (Net income / Revenue)	16.8%		
ROA (Net income / Total assets)	6.7%		
ROE (Net income / Total stockholders' equity)	12.2%		
Asset turnover (Revenue / Total assets)	0.40		

For each ratio, (a) circle the stronger company ratio, (b) place a box around any company ratio that is stronger than the industry norm, and (c) c*omment* on the results.

Q6   The income statement indicates (**strengthening / steady / weakening**) earnings potential. Why? *Comment* on your observations.

STATEMENT OF CASH FLOWS

Q7   The primary source of cash was (**operating / investing / financing**), which is a(n) (**favorable / unfavorable**) sign.

For property, plant, and equipment a *net* cash (**inflow / outflow**) was reported in the (**operating / investing / financing**) activity section so PPE was (**purchased / sold**), which is a(n) (**favorable / unfavorable**) sign *indicating …*

A *net cash inflow for debt* occurred during fye (**2005 / 2004 / 2003 / 2002**), indicating more debt was (**borrowed / repaid**). These amounts appear to have primarily financed (**operations / the purchase of PPE / the repurchase of common stock**).

A *net cash inflow for capital stock* occurred during fye (**2005 / 2004 / 2003 / 2002**), indicating more capital stock was (**issued / repurchased**). This is a(n) (**favorable / unfavorable**) sign *indicating …*

Q8   Net cash from operating activities (**increased / decreased**) by $_____ million or _____%.
During the same time period, dividends paid (**increased / decreased**) by _____%.

Q9   Compute the ratios in the chart below. *For ratio formulas and explanation refer to Appendix B – Ratios.*

CARNIVAL CORPORATION	Industry Norm	Fye 11/30/2005	Fye 11/30/2003
Free cash flow	NA	$	$
Cash flow adequacy ratio	NA		
Cash flow liquidity ratio	NA		
Quality of income ratio	NA		

For each ratio, (a) circle the stronger company ratio and (b) c*omment* on the results.

Q10 Complete the sources and uses of cash and common-size information below for the fye 11/30/2005. Only select accounts are reported below, so amounts may not total.

SOURCES AND USES OF CASH (CCL) COMMON-SIZE STATEMENTS				
Fiscal year ended...	11/30/2005	11/30/2005	11/30/2003	11/30/2003
Net cash from operating activities (NCOA)	$	%	$1,933.0	47.94%
Issuance of debt		%	1,751.0	43.43%
Issuance of capital stock		%	42.0	1.04%
TOTAL Sources of cash	**$4,377.0**	**100.00%**	**$4,032.0**	**100.00%**
Purchase of property, plant, and equipment		%	(2,516.0)	(62.40)%
Repayment of debt		%	(898.0)	(22.27)%
Repurchase of capital stock		%	0.0	0.00%
Cash dividends paid		%	(292.0)	(7.24)%
TOTAL Uses of cash	**($3,842.0)**	**(87.78)%**	**($3,729.0)**	**(92.49)%**
Net change in cash	**$ 535.0**	**12.22%**	**$ 303.0**	**7.51%**

During fye 11/30/2003 the primary sources of cash was _____ contributing _____% and the primary use of cash was _____ using _____% of the total sources of cash.

Q11 The statement of cash flows indicates (**strengthening / steady / weakening**) cash position. Why? *Comment* on your observations.

STATEMENT OF RETAINED EARNINGS

Q12 Complete the statement of retained earnings below.

CARNIVAL CORPORATION (CCL) STATEMENT OF RETAINED EARNINGS ($ in millions)				
Fiscal year ended...	11/30/2005	11/30/2004	11/30/2003	11/30/2002
RE, beginning	$8,623	$7,191	$6,326	$5,556
NI				1,016.0
Dividends				(246.0)
Other adjustments	(81.0)	(22.0)	(37.0)	(0.3)
RE, ending	$	$	$	$6,326

Net income is initially reported on the (**balance sheet / income statement / statement of cash flows**) and dividends paid are initially reported on the (**balance sheet / income statement / statement of cash flows**).

OTHER

Q13 Based on the financial statements presented for Carnival Company, would you invest in this company? (**Yes / No**) Why? *Support* your response with at least five good observations.

TEST YOUR UNDERSTANDING
Comprehensive Analysis

Purpose:
· Analyze the income statement, the balance sheet, and the statement of cash flows
· Prepare a statement of retained earnings

CIRCUIT CITY STORES (CC)	BALANCE SHEET	($ in millions)		
ASSETS	2/28/2006	2/28/2005	2/28/2004	2/28/2003
Cash and cash equivalents	$ 316.0	$ 879.7	$ 783.5	$ 884.7
Short-term investments	522.0	125.3	0.0	0.0
Accounts receivable	220.9	230.6	170.6	140.4
Inventories	1,698.0	1,455.2	1,517.3	1,409.7
Other current assets	76.5	54.4	447.8	653.1
TOTAL Current assets	**2,833.4**	**2,745.2**	**2,919.2**	**3,087.9**
Property, plant, and equipment	2,018.8	1,819.5	1,741.7	1,600.8
Accumulated depreciation	(1,179.4)	(1,092.6)	(1,064.6)	(951.2)
PPE, net	**839.4**	**726.9**	**677.1**	**649.6**
Goodwill	254.4	247.2	0.0	0.0
Long-term investments	0.0	0.0	0.0	0.0
Other non-current assets	142.0	120.7	134.4	103.8
TOTAL Other	**396.4**	**367.9**	**134.4**	**103.8**
TOTAL ASSETS	**$4,069.2**	**$3,840.0**	**$3,730.7**	**$3,841.3**
Accounts payable	$ 850.4	$ 635.7	$ 833.8	$ 963.7
Short-term debt	22.0	0.0	0.0	0.0
Current portion of long-term debt	7.2	0.9	1.1	1.4
Accrued expenses	202.3	170.6	149.6	113.9
Other current liabilities	540.4	508.3	153.7	196.0
TOTAL Current liabilities	**1,622.3**	**1,315.5**	**1,138.2**	**1,275.0**
Long-term debt	52.0	19.9	22.7	11.3
Deferred income taxes	0.0	0.0	0.0	0.0
Other non-current liabilities	440.1	424.7	345.7	181.1
TOTAL Long-term liabilities	**492.1**	**444.6**	**368.4**	**192.4**
TOTAL Liabilities	**2,114.4**	**1,760.1**	**1,506.6**	**1,467.4**
Preferred stock	0.0	0.0	0.0	0.0
Common stock, par	87.4	94.1	102.0	105.0
Additional paid-in capital	458.2	721.0	922.6	965.6
Retained earnings	1,364.7	1,239.7	1,199.4	1,303.3
Other stockholders' equity	44.3	25.1	0.0	0.0
Treasury stock	0.0	0.0	0.0	0.0
TOTAL Stockholders' equity	**1,954.6**	**2,079.9**	**2,224.0**	**2,373.9**
TOTAL L & SE	**$4,069.0**	**$3,840.0**	**$3,730.6**	**$3,841.3**

CIRCUIT CITY STORES (CC)   INCOME STATEMENT   ($ in millions)

Fiscal year ended...	2/28/2006	2/28/2005	2/28/2004	2/28/2003
Revenue	$11,597.0	$10,469.5	$9,857.1	$10,054.9
Cost of goods sold	8,766.8	7,901.4	7,573.0	7,648.0
Gross profit	**2,830.2**	**2,568.1**	**2,284.1**	**2,406.9**
SGA exp	2,439.9	2,321.5	2,117.3	2,237.0
Depreciation/amortization expense	163.8	153.9	197.6	159.8
Other operating expenses (revenues)	(19.4)	(15.0)	(35.0)	13.8
Operating expenses (other than COGS)	2,584.3	2,460.4	2,279.9	2,410.6
Income from operations	**245.9**	**107.7**	**4.2**	**(3.7)**
Interest income (expense)	(6.8)	(4.9)	(5.4)	(1.8)
Other revenues (expenses)	0.0	0.0	0.0	0.0
Income from continuing oper B4 inc tax	**239.1**	**102.8**	**(1.2)**	**(5.5)**
Provision for income taxes	88.0	38.4	(0.4)	(0.2)
Income from continuing operations	**151.1**	**64.4**	**(0.8)**	**(5.3)**
Nonrecurring items	(11.4)	(2.7)	(88.5)	65.3
Net income	**$ 139.7**	**$ 61.7**	**($ 89.3)**	**$ 60.0**
Outstanding shares (in millions)	796	785	789	777

CIRCUIT CITY STORES (CC)   STATEMENT OF CASH FLOWS   ($ in millions)

Fiscal year ended...	2/28/2006	2/28/2005	2/28/2004	2/28/2003
Net income (loss)	$139.7	$ 61.7	($89.3)	$ 60.0
Depreciation/amortization expense	163.8	153.9	197.6	159.8
Deferred income tax	(14.3)	(116.5)	(35.6)	(18.7)
Operating (gains) losses	27.4	16.7	120.2	(48.9)
Changes in working capital	38.5	335.8	(75.8)	(395.1)
Net cash from operating activities (NCOA)	**$355.1**	**$451.6**	**$117.1**	**($242.9)**
Sale of property, plant, equipment	55.4	582.2	46.6	60.9
Sale of investments	1,014.9	0.0	0.0	0.0
Purchase of property, plant, and equipment	(254.5)	(538.0)	(175.8)	(150.8)
Purchase of investments	(1,409.8)	(125.3)	0.0	0.0
Other investing cash flow items	(8.0)	0.0	0.0	0.0
Net cash from investing activities (NCIA)	**($602.0)**	**($81.1)**	**($129.2)**	**($89.9)**
Issuance of debt	77.0	0.0	0.0	0.0
Issuance of capital stock	38.0	27.1	11.5	9.2
Repayment of debt	(57.7)	(29.9)	(1.5)	(25.3)
Repurchase of capital stock	(338.5)	(259.8)	(84.4)	0.0
Cash dividends paid	(12.8)	(13.8)	(14.7)	(14.7)
Other financing cash flow items	(24.4)	0.0	0.0	0.0
Net cash from financing activities (NCFA)	**($318.4)**	**($276.4)**	**($89.1)**	**($30.8)**
Effect of exchange rate changes	1.6	2.1	0.0	0.0
Net change in cash	**(563.7)**	**96.2**	**(101.2)**	**(363.6)**
+ Beginning cash and cash equivalents	879.7	783.5	884.7	1,248.2
= Ending cash and cash equivalents	$316.0	$879.7	$783.5	$884.6
Cash interest paid	$ 6.8	$ 4.9	$ 5.4	$ 1.8
Cash taxes paid	$ 94.2	$ 152.8	$ 36.3	$ 107.9
Free cash flow	$ 87.8	($100.2)	($73.4)	($408.4)

Refer to the financial statements presented for Circuit City on the previous two pages to answer the following questions.

BALANCE SHEET

Q1 (1) Examine the following accounts, subtotals, and totals; (2) describe your observations; and then (3) identify what your observations indicate. A response is given for Cash and Short-term investments to help with understanding.

a. Cash and Short-term investments ... *cash decreased and short-term investments increased resulting in the total remaining approximately constant, indicating that the company is trying to better manage its cash by investing idle cash in short-term investments.*

b. Inventory ...

c. Total assets ...

d. Contributed capital totaled $_____ million on 2/28/2006 ...

e. Retained earnings...

Q2 Compute the ratios in the chart below. *For ratio formulas and explanation refer to Appendix B – Ratios.*

CIRCUIT CITY	*Industry Norm*	2/28/2006	2/28/2003
Current ratio (CA / CL)	*1.5*		
Quick ratio (Cash + ST Invest+ AR / CL)	*0.6*		
Debt ratio (Total liabilities / Total assets)	*0.19*		
Times Interest Earned (Inc from oper / Int exp)	*3.5*		

For each ratio, (a) compare the two years of company ratios and circle the stronger ratio, (b) place a box around any company ratio that is stronger than the industry norm, and (c) c*omment* on the results.

Q3 The balance sheet indicates a (**strengthening** / **steady** / **weakening**) financial position. Why? *Comment* on your observations.

INCOME STATEMENT

Q4 Revenues were $_____ million for the earliest year reported and $_____ million for the most recent year reported. Since the earliest year reported, this account has (**increased** / **decreased**) by $_____ million, which is a _____% (**increase** / **decrease**). During the same time period, COGS (**increased** / **decreased**) by _____%, operating expenses (other than COGS) (**increased** / **decreased**) by _____%, and net income (**increased** / **decreased**) by _____%.

Q5 Compute the ratios in the chart below. *For ratio formulas and explanation refer to Appendix B – Ratios.*

CIRCUIT CITY	Industry Norm	Fye 2/28/2006	Fye 2/28/2003
Gross profit margin (Gross profit / Revenue)	24.0%		
ROS (Net income / Revenue)	3.4%		
ROA (Net income / Total assets)	9.5%		
ROE (Net income / Total stockholders' equity)	20.5%		
Accounts receivable turnover (Revenue / AR)	81.9		
Inventory turnover (COGS / Inventory)	6.2		
Asset turnover (Revenue / Total assets)	2.8		

For each ratio, (a) circle the stronger company ratio, (b) place a box around any company ratio that is stronger than the industry norm, and (c) c*omment* on the results.

Q6 The income statement and the above ratios indicate (**strengthening / steady / weakening**) earnings potential. Why? *Comment* on your observations.

STATEMENT OF CASH FLOWS

Q7 The primary source of cash was operating activities during fye (**2006 / 2005 / 2004 / 2003**).

A *net cash outflow for PPE* occurred during fye (**2006 / 2005 / 2004 / 2003**), *indicating …*

A *net cash inflow for short-term investments* occurred during fye (**2006 / 2005 / 2004 / 2003**), *indicating …*

A *net cash outflow for capital stock* occurred during fye (**2006 / 2005 / 2004 / 2003**), meaning more capital stock was (**issued / repurchased**). Repurchased common stock is referred to as (**common / preferred / treasury**) stock and it (**increases / decreases**) total stockholders' equity on the balance sheet. This is (**favorable / unfavorable**) for shareholders because earnings per share (**increases / decreases**).

Q8 Compute the ratios in the chart below. *For ratio formulas and explanation refer to Appendix B – Ratios.*

CIRCUIT CITY	Industry Norm	2006	2003
Free cash flow	NA	$	$
Cash flow adequacy ratio	NA		
Cash flow liquidity ratio	NA		
Quality of income ratio	NA		

For each ratio, (a) circle the stronger company ratio and (b) c*omment* on the results.

Q9   Complete the missing information in the sources and uses of cash statement below for fye 2/28/2006.

CIRCUIT CITY STORES (CC) SOURCES AND USES OF CASH ($ in millions)				
Fiscal year ended...	2/28/2006	2/28/2005	2/28/2004	2/28/2003
Net cash from operating activities (NCOA)	$_____	$ 451.6	$117.1	$_____
Sale of property, plant, equipment		582.2	46.6	60.9
Sale of investments		0.0	0.0	0.0
Issuance of debt		0.0	0.0	0.0
Issuance of capital stock		27.1	11.5	9.2
Effect of exchange rate changes		2.1	0.0	0.0
TOTAL Sources of cash	1,542.0	1,063.0	175.2	70.1
TOTAL Uses of cash	(2,105.7)	(966.8)	(276.4)	(190.8)
Net change in cash	($ 563.7)	$ 96.2	($101.2)	($120.7)

Q10   The statement of cash flows indicates adequate cash during fye (2006 / 2005 / 2004 / 2003) and a.
(strengthening / steady / weakening) cash position. Why? *Comment* on your observations.

STATEMENT OF RETAINED EARNINGS

Q11   Complete the statement of retained earnings below.

CIRCUIT CITY STORES (CC) STATEMENT OF RETAINED EARNINGS ($ in millions)				
Fiscal year ended...	2/28/2006	2/28/2005	2/28/2004	2/28/2003
RE, Beginning	$1,239.7	$1,199.4	$1,303.3	$1,801.6
Net income				60.0
Dividends paid				(14.7)
Other adjustments	(1.9)	(7.6)	0.1	(543.6)
RE, ending	$	$	$	$1,303.3

a.   A net loss was reported during fye (2006 / 2005 / 2004 / 2003) and dividends decreased during
fye (2006 / 2005 / 2004 / 2003). What might be one reason that dividends paid decreased?

b.   Retained earnings decreased during fye (2006 / 2005 / 2004 / 2003). *Why?*

OTHER

Q12   Based on the financial statements presented for Circuit City, would you invest in this company?
(Yes / No)   Why? *Support* your response with at least five good observations.

TEST YOUR UNDERSTANDING
Comprehensive Analysis

Purpose:
- Analyze the income statement, the balance sheet, and the statement of cash flows
- Prepare a statement of retained earnings

GOOGLE BALANCE SHEET ($ in millions)				
ASSETS	**12/31/2005**	**12/31/2004**	**12/31/2003**	**12/31/2002**
Cash and cash equivalents	$ 3,877.2	$ 426.9	$149.0	$ 57.8
Short-term investments	4,157.1	1,705.4	185.7	88.6
Accounts receivable	688.0	382.3	154.7	62.0
Inventories	0.0	0.0	0.0	0.0
Other current assets	278.8	178.9	70.8	23.4
TOTAL Current assets	**9,001.1**	**2,693.5**	**560.2**	**231.8**
Property, plant, and equipment	1,417.4	583.1	261.9	86.9
Accumulated depreciation	(455.7)	(204.2)	(73.6)	(33.0)
PPE, net	**961.7**	**378.9**	**188.3**	**53.9**
Goodwill	194.9	122.8	87.4	0.0
Intangibles	82.8	71.1	18.2	0.1
Other non-current assets	31.3	47.1	17.4	1.1
TOTAL Other	**309.0**	**241.0**	**123.0**	**1.2**
TOTAL ASSETS	**$10,271.8**	**$3,313.4**	**$871.5**	**$286.9**
Accounts payable	$ 115.6	$ 32.7	$ 46.2	$ 9.4
Short-term debt	0.0	0.0	0.0	0.0
Current portion of long-term debt	0.0	1.9	4.6	4.4
Accrued expenses	528.9	269.3	148.6	38.4
Other current liabilities	100.9	36.5	36.1	37.3
TOTAL Current liabilities	**745.4**	**340.4**	**235.5**	**89.5**
Long-term debt	0.0	0.0	2.0	6.5
Deferred income taxes	35.4	0.0	18.5	0.6
Other non-current liabilities	72.1	43.9	12.8	2.5
TOTAL Long-term liabilities	**107.5**	**43.9**	**33.3**	**9.6**
TOTAL Liabilities	**852.9**	**384.3**	**268.8**	**99.1**
Preferred stock	0.0	0.0	58.2	58.2
Common stock, par	0.3	0.3	0.2	0.1
Additional paid-in capital	7,477.8	2,582.4	725.2	83.4
Retained earnings	2,055.9	590.5	191.4	85.7
Other stockholders' equity	(115.1)	(244.1)	(372.3)	(39.6)
Treasury stock	0.0	0.0	0.0	0.0
TOTAL Stockholders' equity	**9,418.9**	**2,929.1**	**602.7**	**187.8**
TOTAL L & SE	**$10,271.8**	**$3,313.4**	**$871.5**	**$286.9**

GOOGLE   INCOME STATEMENT   ($ in millions)

	2005	2004	2003	2002
Revenue	$6,138.6	$3,189.2	$1,465.9	$439.5
Cost of goods sold	2,571.5	1,457.6	625.8	131.5
Gross profit	**3,567.1**	**1,731.6**	**840.1**	**308.0**
SGA exp	682.0	516.3	356.2	71.8
Research & development	484.0	225.6	91.2	31.7
Depreciation/amortization expense	293.8	148.4	50.2	18.0
Other operating expenses (revenues)	90.0	201.1	0.0	0.0
Total operating expenses (other than COGS)	1,549.8	1,091.4	497.6	121.5
Income from operations	**2,017.3**	**640.2**	**342.5**	**186.5**
Interest income (expense)	(0.8)	(0.9)	(1.9)	(2.6)
Other revenues (expenses)	125.2	10.9	6.1	1.0
Income from continuing oper B4 inc tax	**2,141.7**	**650.2**	**346.7**	**184.9**
Provision for income taxes	676.3	251.1	241.1	85.2
Income from continuing operations	**1,465.4**	**399.1**	**105.6**	**99.7**
Nonrecurring items	0.0	0.0	0.0	0.0
Net income	**$1,465.4**	**$ 399.1**	**$ 105.6**	**$ 99.7**
Outstanding shares (in millions)	275.84	193.18	137.70	115.24

GOOGLE   STATEMENT OF CASH FLOWS   ($ in millions)

	2005	2004	2003	2002
Net income (loss)	$1,465.4	$399.1	$105.6	$ 99.7
Depreciation/amortization expense	293.8	148.4	50.2	18.0
Deferred income tax	0.0	0.0	0.0	(9.9)
Operating (gains) losses	656.5	682.7	245.8	32.6
Changes in working capital	43.7	(253.2)	(6.2)	14.9
Net cash from operating activities (NCOA)	**$2,459.4**	**$977.0**	**$395.4**	**$155.3**
Sale of property, plant, equipment	0.0	0.0	0.0	0.0
Sale of investments	10,257.2	2,611.1	219.4	20.4
Purchase of property, plant, and equipment	(939.5)	(341.0)	(216.8)	(37.2)
Purchase of investments	(12,675.9)	(4,134.6)	(316.6)	(93.1)
Other investing cash flow items	0.0	(36.9)	0.0	0.1
Net cash from investing activities (NCIA)	**($3,358.2)**	**($1,901.4)**	**($314.0)**	**($109.8)**
Issuance of debt	0.0	0.0	0.0	0.0
Issuance of capital stock	4,372.2	1,195.0	15.5	2.2
Repayment of debt	(1.4)	(4.7)	(7.4)	(7.7)
Repurchase of capital stock	0.0	0.0	0.0	0.0
Cash dividends paid	0.0	0.0	0.0	0.0
Other financing cash flow items	0.0	4.3	0.0	0.0
Net cash from financing activities (NCFA)	**$4,370.8**	**$1,194.6**	**$ 8.1**	**($ 5.5)**
Effect of exchange rate changes	(21.7)	7.7	1.7	0.1
Net change in cash	**3,450.3**	**277.9**	**91.2**	**40.1**
+ Beginning cash and cash equivalents	426.9	149.0	57.8	17.7
= Ending cash and cash equivalents	$3,877.2	$ 426.9	$149.0	$ 57.8
Cash interest paid	$ 0.2	$ 0.7	$ 1.7	$ 2.3
Cash taxes paid	$ 153.6	$ 183.8	$247.4	$ 73.8
Free cash flow	$1,519.9	$ 636.0	$178.6	$118.1

Refer to the financial statements presented for Google Inc. on the previous two pages to answer the following questions.

BALANCE SHEET

Q1 (1) Examine the following accounts, subtotals, and totals; (2) describe your observations; and then (3) identify what your observations indicate. A response is given for Cash and Short-term investments to help with understanding.

a.   Cash and Short-term investments … *have increased dramatically since 2002 and in 2005 comprise 78% of Total Assets, indicating a company that is rich in cash.*

b.   Total assets …

c.   Contributed capital totaled $_____ million on 12/31/2005 …

d.   Retained earnings...

Q2 Compute the ratios in the chart below. *For ratio formulas and explanation refer to Appendix B – Ratios.*

GOOGLE INC.	*Industry Norm*	12/31/2005	12/31/2002
Current ratio (CA / CL)	8.5		
Quick ratio (Cash + ST Invest+ AR / CL)	8.5		
Debt ratio (Total liabilities / Total assets)	0.04		
Times Interest Earned (Inc from oper / Int exp)	4.6		

For each ratio, (a) circle the stronger company ratio, (b) place a box around any company ratio that is stronger than the industry norm, and (c) c*omment* on the results.

Q3 The balance sheet indicates a (**strengthening** / **steady** / **weakening**) financial position. Why? *Comment* on your observations.

INCOME STATEMENT

Q4 Compute the ratios in the chart below. *For ratio formulas and explanation refer to Appendix B – Ratios.*

GOOGLE INC.	*Industry Norm*	2005	2002
ROA (Net income / Total assets)	18.0%		
ROE (See Appendix B for the ratio formula)	20.9%		
Accounts receivable turnover (Revenue / AR)	11.6		
A/R days (360 days in the year / AR turnover)	31		

For each ratio, (a) circle the stronger company ratio, (b) place a box around any company ratio that is stronger than the industry norm, and (c) c*omment* on the results.

Q5 Compute the missing information for 2005 in the common-size statements below.

GOOGLE Common-size Statements	2005	2004	2003	2002
Revenue	%	100.0%	100.0%	100.0%
Cost of goods sold	%	45.7%	42.7%	29.9%
Operating expenses	%	34.2%	33.9%	27.6%
Other revenues (expenses)	%	0.3%	0.3%	-0.4%
Provision for income taxes	%	7.9%	16.4%	19.4%
Net income	23.9%	12.5%	7.2%	22.7%

    a.   Gross profit margin (gross profit / revenue) was _____% in 2005, _____% in 2004, _____% in 2003, and _____% in 2002, which is a(n) (**increasing** / **decreasing**) trend resulting from an increase in (**revenues** / **COGS** / **operating expenses**).

    b.   ROS (net income / revenue) was _____% in 2005, _____% in 2004, _____% in 2003, and _____% in 2002. The low ROS during 2003 and 2004 result from an (**increase** / **decrease**) in (**revenues** / **COGS** / **operating expenses**).

Q6 The income statement and the above ratios indicate (**strengthening** / **steady** / **weakening**) earnings potential. Why? *Comment* on your observations.

STATEMENT OF CASH FLOWS

Q7 The primary source of cash was operating activities during (**2005** / **2004** / **2003** / **2002**).

A *net cash outflow for PPE* occurred during (**2005** / **2004** / **2003** / **2002**), indicating ...

A *net cash inflow for short-term investments* occurred during (**2005** / **2004** / **2003** / **2002**), *indicating* ...

A *net cash inflow for capital stock* occurred during (**2005** / **2004** / **2003** / **2002**) meaning more capital stock was (**issued** / **repurchased**), *indicating* ...

Q8 Compute the ratios in the chart below. *For ratio formulas and explanation refer to Appendix B – Ratios.*

CIRCUIT CITY	*Industry Norm*	2006	2003
Free cash flow	*NA*	$	$
Cash flow adequacy ratio	*NA*		
Cash flow liquidity ratio	*NA*		
Quality of income ratio	*NA*		

For each ratio, (a) circle the stronger company ratio and (b) c*omment* on the results.

Q9 Complete the missing information in the sources and uses of cash statement below for 2005.

SOURCES AND USES OF CASH				
	2005	**2004**	**2003**	**2002**
Net cash from operating activities	$	$ 977.0	$395.4	$155.3
Sale of property, plant, equipment		0.0	0.0	0.0
Sale of investments		2,611.1	219.4	20.4
Other investing cash flow items			0.0	0.1
Issuance of debt		0.0	0.0	0.0
Issuance of capital stock		1,195.0	15.5	2.2
Other financing cash flow items			0.0	
Effect of exchange rate changes		7.7	1.7	0.1
TOTAL Sources of cash	**$17,088.8**	**$4,790.8**	**$632.0**	**$178.1**
Purchase of property, plant, and equipment	$	($341.0)	($216.8)	($37.2)
Purchase of investments		(4,134.6)	(316.6)	(93.1)
Other investing cash flow items		(36.9)	0.0	0.0
Repayment of debt		(4.7)	(7.4)	(7.7)
Repurchase of capital stock		0.0	0.0	0.0
Cash dividends paid		0.0	0.0	0.0
Other financing cash flow items		4.3		0.0
Effect of exchange rate changes				
TOTAL Uses of cash	**($13,638.5)**	**($4,512.9)**	**($540.8)**	**($138.0)**
Net change in cash	**$ 3,450.3**	**$ 277.9**	**$ 91.2**	**$ 40.1**

Q10 The statement of cash flows indicates adequate cash during (2003 / 2004 / 2005 / 2006) and a. (strengthening / steady / weakening) cash position. *Comment* on your observations.

STATEMENT OF RETAINED EARNINGS

Q11 Complete the statement of retained earnings below.

GOOGLE STATEMENT OF RETAINED EARNINGS ($ in millions)				
	2005	**2004**	**2003**	**2002**
RE, beginning	$	$	$	$ 0.7
Net income				99.7
Dividends paid				0.0
Other adjustments	0.0	0.0	0.1	(14.7)
RE, ending	$	$	$	$85.7

Does Google pay dividends? (Yes / No)   If not, why not?

OTHER

Q12 Based on the financial statements presented for Google Inc., would you invest in this company? (Yes / No)   Why? *Support* your response with at least five good observations.

CHAPTER 7 – CORPORATE ANALYSIS

PURPOSE: This chapter outlines a capstone project that includes researching and analyzing a publicly traded corporation of the student's choice. This project is divided into six parts. In Part I, students research and describe their company's primary business activities in addition to providing information regarding the company's history, position within their industry, competition, recent developments, and future direction. In Part II a ten-year market analysis is completed. Part III requires research into industry norms for commonly used ratios. In Part IV the corporate financial statements are analyzed using trend analysis and common-size statement techniques. Parts V and VI ask the student to answer the question, "Would you advise a friend to invest in this company?" Each part requires at least a one-page written analysis. These analyses must be individually written with each student submitting a separate report.

Have fun with this project! Be creative! Include graphs, charts, and other items to enhance the overall project.

If you are undecided regarding which company to select, below is a listing of the 30 corporations comprising the Dow Jones Industrial Average (DJIA) plus other corporations that you may find of interest.

"30 INDUSTRIAL" STOCKS
that currently comprise the
DOW JONES INDUSTRIAL AVERAGE

ALCOA (AA)	COCA COLA (KO)	HONEYWELL (HON)	PFIZER (PFE)
AMER INTL GROUP (AIG)	Walt DISNEY (DIS)	IBM (IBM)	PROCTER & GAMBLE (PG)
ALTRIA GRP (MO)	DUPONT (DD)	INTEL (INTC)	SBC COMM (SBC)
AMERICAN EXPRESS (AXP)	EXXON MOBIL (XOM)	JOHNSON & JOHNSON (JNJ)	3M (MMM)
BOEING (BA)	General ELECTRIC (GE)	JP MORGAN CHASE (JPM)	UNITED TECHNOLOGIES (UTX)
(CAT)ERPILLAR	General MOTORS (GM)	MCDONALDS (MCD)	WAL-MART (WMT)
CITIGROUP (C)	HEWLETT-PACKARD (HPQ)	MERCK (MRK)	VERIZON COMM (VZ)
	HOME DEPOT (HD)	MICROSOFT (MSFT)	

OTHER CORPORATIONS

Advanced Micro Devices	eBay	Lilly (Eli)	Qualcomm
Amazon.com	FedEx Corp	Liz Claiborne	Royal Caribbean Cruises
American Greetings	Ford Motor Co	Lockheed Martin	Reebok International
American Home Products	Fossil, Inc.	LSI Logic	Sara Lee
Amgen	Gannett	Lucent Technologies	Sears, Roebuck & Co
AMR (American Airlines)	Gap, Inc. (The)	Mattel	Southwest Airlines
Anheuser-Busch	General Mills	May Dept Stores	Starbucks
Barnes & Noble, Inc.	Gillette	MCI	Sun Microsystems
Best Buy	Google	Monsanto	Toys R Us
Borders Group	Harley-Davidson	Motorola	Walgreen Co
Brinker International	Hasbro	Nike Inc.	Waste Management
Bristol-Meyers Squibb	Hershey Foods	Office Depot	Wrigley (Wm.) Jr.
Callaway Golf	Heinz (HJ)	Oracle	Xerox Corp
Carnival Company	IHOP	Outback Steakhouse	Yahoo! Inc
Circuit City Stores	Kimberly-Clark	Panera Bread	Yum! Brand
Costco Wholesale	Kmart	Papa John's	
Deckers Outdoor	Kellogg	PepsiCo	
Dell Computer	Kroger	Pfizer	
Dow Chemical	Lauder (Estee)	Pitney Bowes	

Activity 71   **PART I:**   **TELL ME ABOUT YOUR COMPANY**

Purpose: ·   Use a variety of resources to research a corporation
                 ·   Prepare a well-written paper describing your corporation

Choose a company to research. The company must be publicly traded, not the company you currently work for, and not in a regulated industry. Your selection may be a competitor or a supplier of your company, related to a hobby of yours, a possible stock investment, or simply sound interesting.

Each student will select a different company, however, companies may be within the same industry. The instructor must approve the company.

Requirements:

A.   **Research and then describe your company's primary business activities.** Also include a brief historical summary, a list of competitors, the company's position within the industry, recent developments within the company/industry, future direction, and other items of significance to your corporation.

B.   **Include information from a variety of resources.**
      1.   **Consult the Form 10-K filed with the SEC.** This form contains a wealth of information. Read through *Item 1. Business Summary* to locate information regarding the business, product offerings, marketing strategy, competition, and market share. Available at www.sec.gov.
      2.   **Review the Annual Report** and be certain to read through the *Letter to Shareholders,* which summarizes the past year and highlights future opportunities. Annual Reports are generally available online at the company's website in the investor relations section.
      3.   **Explore the corporate website**. A corporate website usually provides updated, comprehensive information including links to current news items and financial information. Note that the company provides the information posted on the website, and therefore, may be biased in favor of the company.
      4.   **Select *at least two* significant news items from recent business periodicals**. Examples of business periodicals include *The Wall Street Journal, Forbes, Fortune, Inc.,* and *Business Week.* Many of these periodicals are available at the library in hard copy and also online.
      5.   **Use information from *at least one* financial service**:
           Library references: *The Value Line Investment Survey, Standard and Poor's Stock Reports or Industry Surveys, Mergent's Industry Review*
           Free Internet resources: finance.yahoo.com, moneycentral.msn.com, www.hoovers.com, and other financial websites

           These services provide a historical summary, description of the primary business activities, recent developments, and select financial information about publicly-traded companies.

C.   **Submit a "Tell Me About Your Company" report that is two to five pages long**. The report should be well written with introductory and concluding paragraphs. References must be appropriately cited. *Format*: Double-spaced, one-inch margins, using a 12-point Times-New-Roman font.

D.   **In the appendix**, appropriately identify and place photocopies or a computer printout of the material used for your report noting the source. Highlight significant information. Incorporate this information into your report.

PART II: STOCK MARKET RESEARCH

Purpose: ·   Research the current stock quote of your company and analyze past market activity
                 ·   Summarize stock market activity results

Requirements:

A.   **Research the stock market** activity of your company's stock, including the current stock quote and market activity over the most recent 10 years.

B.   **Summarize the results in a one-page report.**
       Format: Double-spaced, one-inch margins, using a 12-point Times-New-Roman font.

C.   **In the appendix**, appropriately identify and place photocopies or a computer printout of the material used for your report noting the source. Highlight significant information.

PART III: **COMPUTE RATIOS AND COMPARE TO INDUSTRY NORMS**

Purpose:
- Research the primary SIC (Standard Industrial Classification) Code for your company
- Use resources available to obtain industry averages for commonly used ratios
- Compare company ratio results to industry averages
- Prepare a well-written report summarizing the ratio analysis using appropriate business and accounting vocabulary

Requirements:

A. **Obtain the four-digit primary SIC (Standard Industrial Classification) Code and industry title for your company.** Record the primary SIC code and industry title at the top of the Ratio Analysis Worksheet. The Standard Industrial Classification code is a coding system used to report information on U.S. businesses. It divides corporations into 10 major groups that are further divided into major categories. Many corporations engage in more than one type of business. Within a company, the primary SIC code refers to the type of business with the largest volume of sales. Secondary SIC codes are listed in descending order according to sales volume. The first page of the Form 10-K displays the primary SIC Code within the initial company information available at www.sec.gov.

B. **Obtain industry averages for commonly used ratios.** Industry average information is reported by industry title or SIC code. Record the industry averages available for your company in the first column of the Ratios Analysis Worksheet. Resources for industry average information include:

Free online references include *finance.yahoo.com* and *moneycentral.msn.com.*
Printed library references include *Almanac of Business and Industrial Financial Ratios*, by Leo Troy, published by Prentice Hall, *Industry Norms and Key Business Ratios*, Dun and Bradstreet, Inc., *Standard and Poor's Industry Surveys,* and *Mergent's Industry Review.*

C. **Obtain or calculate the ratios listed on the Ratio Analysis Worksheet for the three most recent years of information.** Use the attached forms or facsimiles. Free online references include *finance.yahoo.com, moneycentral.msn.com,* and edgarscan.pwcglobal.com/servlets/edgarscan.

D. **Submit a report that is at least one page long.** The report should be a well-written paper that (1) comments on significant amounts, trends, and relationships of the three years of ratio information, (2) compares company ratios to industry averages, and (3) summarizes and comments on the information using the categories: liquidity, long-term solvency, management efficiency, profitability, and investment ratios.

Format: Double-spaced, one-inch margins, using a 12-point Times-New-Roman font.

E. **In the appendix**, appropriately identify and place photocopies or a computer printout of the industry average and ratio information used for your report noting the source. Include any manual computations of the corporate ratios. Highlight significant information.

Activity 74   **PART IV: PREPARE FINANCIAL STATEMENTS IN CONDENSED FORMAT AND A WRITTEN ANALYSIS**

Purpose:
- Use resources available to obtain financial statements for the past four fiscal years
- Prepare a classified balance sheet, multi-step income statement, and the statement of cash flows using the condensed format provided
- Prepare a sources and uses of cash statement
- Prepare trend analyses and common-size statements
- Prepare a well-written analysis of each financial statement using appropriate business and accounting vocabulary

Requirements:

A.   **Obtain the financial statements for the past four fiscal years for the company you selected**. Financial statements are available from a variety of online sources including *finance.yahoo.com*, *moneycentral.msn.com*, edgarscan.pwcglobal.com/servlets/edgarscan, and www.sec.gov.

B.   **Prepare a multi-step income statement, classified balance sheet, and statement of cash flows in condensed format**. Condensed means some accounts are grouped into one summarized subtotal, but no numbers are left out of the computations. Each financial statement should total properly. Use the attached forms or facsimiles.

C.   **Prepare trend analyses and for the income statement, balance sheet, and the statement of cash flows. Prepare common-size statements and for the income statement, balance sheet, and the sources and uses of cash statement**. Use the attached forms or facsimiles.

D.   **Submit at least one page of written analysis for *each* financial statement**. The report should be well written using appropriate business and accounting vocabulary. Comment on significant amounts, trends, and relationships. When appropriate, reference amounts from the trend analyses and common-size statements.

    Format: Double-spaced, one-inch margins, using a 12-point Times-New-Roman font.

E.   **In the appendix**, appropriately identify and place photocopies or a computer printout of the financial statement information used noting the source. Highlight significant information.

Activity 75   **PART V:**   ***WRITTEN REPORT*: WOULD YOU ADVISE A FRIEND TO INVEST IN THIS COMPANY?**

Purpose: · Base a recommendation on previous research, analysis, and sound reasoning
                 · Prepare a well-written report using appropriate business and accounting vocabulary

Requirements:

A.   Prepare a written report titled **"Would you advise a friend to invest in this company?"** based upon your research and analysis of this company's financial information. Identify 3-5 significant points that justify your conclusion. Support your points with a comprehensive explanation incorporating sound reasoning.

B.   **Submit a report that is 1-2 pages long.** The report should be well written with introductory and concluding paragraphs. References must be appropriately cited.
       Format: Double-spaced, one-inch margins, using a 12-point Times-New-Roman font.

Activity 76   **PART VI: PRESENTATION: WOULD YOU ADVISE A FRIEND TO INVEST IN THIS COMPANY?**

Purpose: · Base a recommendation on previous research, analysis, and sound reasoning
             · Prepare a presentation using one visual aid

Requirements:

A.   Prepare a presentation titled **"Would you advise a friend to invest in this company?"** based upon your research and analysis of this company's financial information.

- The presentation should present historical, competitive, and financial research that supports advice about investing in your company.
- Share the 3-5 significant points that justify your conclusion -- the significant *highlights* of your research (rather than a summary of all your research findings.)
- The presentation should be delivered well with introductory and concluding paragraphs.
- Please support your fellow students by being attentive and courteous during their presentations.

B.   **Deliver a 5 – 8 minute oral presentation to the class that keeps the attention of the audience.** Five points are awarded for staying within the 5-8 minute time limit, zero points if not. At 8 minutes you will be given a cut-off sign to finish your closing sentence.

C.   **Use at least one visual aid…**PowerPoint slides, props, etc.

D.   **Answer questions of fellow students after your presentation**. Each student should listen attentively to the other presentations and jot down questions. During each *class* of presentations, every student is expected to ask at least one question.

E.   **In the appendix** provide a copy of PowerPoint slides and other written visual aids for the instructor.

APPENDIX

Be creative! Include graphs, charts, pictures, and other items to enhance the overall project. Additional points may be awarded (up to the maximum) for additional information provided and creativity. Remember to also include copies of the documentation requested in Parts I through VI.

PRESENTATION TIPS

1. Opening should grab the audience's attention.
    Opening techniques include asking a question, stating an interesting fact, or telling a story. The story could be about an incident that led you to choose this company to research.

2. Identify 3-5 three main points that you want the audience to remember. Support these points with good explanation and examples.

3. Body: State what you are going to say, say it, and then summarize what you said.

4. A Visual Aid is just that – an aid that supports the presentation.
    If using PowerPoint – no more than one slide per minute (max 8).
    Keep aids uncluttered and readable – no more than 7 items across and 7 items down.

5. Closing is evident and leaves a definite impression.

6. Practice your opening and closing -- as these are critical.

7. Talk to your audience. You may use note cards with key points and key statistics.
    Be careful not to read your presentation.

8. Speak slowly and clearly.
    If you look at the last row your voice will project to the last row.

9. Achieve eye contact with your audience. Look at foreheads if eye contact is intimidating. Plant a smiling friend at the back of the audience for you to look at during the presentation for encouragement.

10. Stand with your feet planted squarely on the ground, not leaning against the podium or swaying back and forth.

11. Please be courteous and attentive during other student presentations. Thank you.

12. Consider the…**P**urpose, **A**udience, **I**nformation, **B**enefits, **O**bjections, **C**ontext

13. If your presentation is videotaped, review the video 5 different times, each time using one of the following techniques. View it…
    a. As yourself
    b. As a boss
    c. With just sound – Listen (turn your back to the screen so that you cannot see the video)
    d. With no sound – Just the visual
    e. With someone else

PART V: WRITTEN PROJECT GRADE SHEET

Name _____ Company _____

POINTS

_____/20   **PART I** (Act 71) Tell me about your company
           Primary business activity
           Historical summary
           Competitors / Position within the industry
           Recent developments and other significant information
           2-5 pages, typed and double-spaced

_____/10   **PART II** (Act 72) Stock market research
           Current stock market activity
           10-year stock market analysis
           One-page summary

_____/ 10   **PART III** (Act 73) Compute ratios and compare to industry norms
           Company ratios
           Industry averages (at least nine, all ratios do not apply to all industries)
           One-page written analysis

                PART IV (Act 74) Prepare financial statements in condensed format and a written analysis
_____/10   *Income Statement*, Trend analysis, Common-size statements
                One-page written analysis
_____/10   *Balance Sheet*, Trend analysis, Common-size statements
                One-page written analysis
_____/10   *Statement of Cash Flows,* Trend analysis
          Sources And Uses Cash Of Statement, Common-size statements
                One-page written analysis
          Typed and double-spaced

_____/ 10   **PART V** (Act 75) Would you advise a friend to invest in this corporation?
           Conclusion supported by sound reasoning
           Comprehensive
           At least 2 pages, typed and double-spaced

_____/ 10   **APPENDIX**   Significant information highlighted
           Part I: 2 news items, 1 financial service resource, and other significant resources
           Part II: Stock market research items
           Part III: Industry average information and ratio computations
           Part IV: Copies of the financial statements

_____/ 10   **OTHER**   10 to 20 pages, not including Appendices
           Good writing style, good grammar, 12-point Times-New-Roman font
           Well-organized, attractive, and creative
           Effective use of graphs and charts

_____/100   **TOTAL SCORE**

PART VI: PRESENTATION GRADE SHEET

Student name:			Company:	

Points Possible	Points Awarded	ITEM	DESCRIPTION
10		OPENING AND CLOSING	Strong opening – vivid and compelling, should grab the audience's attention. Summarize before concluding Closing is evident and leaves a definite impression of your investment advice.
10		AUDIENCE APPEAL	Information benefits the audience and is interesting Audience is attentive and can easily follow
25		CONTENT	Body has a clear purpose -- State what you are going to say, say it, and then summarize what you just said Presents a clear line of reasoning -- Main points are supported with good explanation and examples Knowledgeable about the company/subject Information is accurate Highlights presented, not a summary of the project Well organized Direct link to accounting should be obvious
10		PRESENTATION	Appropriate eye contact with the audience Note cards may be used, but not read Seems confident, relaxed, and in control Uses appropriate gestures, tone, volume, delivery rate Sense of humor Professional appearance
10		VOICE	Voice is projected to the back row Pronounces, enunciates, and speaks well Professional language Few "ums" and "okays" Energetic
10		VISUAL AID (*Please provide a copy for the instructor*)	Uses visual aids to clarify and emphasize content Attractive Not more than 1 PowerPoint slide per minute (max 8) Not cluttered – not more than 7 items across and 7 items down
10		ADVICE	Investing advice is clearly stated and well-supported
0 or 5		TIME LIMIT	5-8 Minutes
10		QUESTION AND ANSWER	Effective, tactful, and thoughtful Student presentations: Ask at least one question per *class* regarding other student presentations.
100		**Total Points**	

Company Name: _____

CONDENSED
CLASSIFIED BALANCE SHEET

Dated: ($ in millions)	_____ (Most recent year)	_____	_____	_____
Current assets	$	$	$	$
Property, plant, and equipment, net				
Other assets				
TOTAL ASSETS	$	$	$	$

Current liabilities	$	$	$	$
Long-term liabilities				
Contributed capital				
Retained earnings				
Treasury stock and other stockholders' equity				
TOTAL L & SE	$	$	$	$

Company Name: _____

CONDENSED CLASSIFIED BALANCE SHEET
Trend Analysis

Dated: ($ in millions)	_____ (Most recent year)	_____	_____	_____
Current assets				100
Property, plant, and equipment, net				100
Other assets				100
TOTAL ASSETS				**100**

Current liabilities				100
Long-term liabilities				100
Contributed capital				100
Retained earnings				100
Treasury stock and other stockholders' equity				100
TOTAL L & SE				**100**

Company Name: _____

CONDENSED CLASSIFIED BALANCE SHEET
Common-Size Statements

Dated: ($ in millions)	_____ (Most recent year)	_____	_____	_____
Current assets	%	%	%	%
Property, plant, and equipment, net	%	%	%	%
Other assets	%	%	%	%
TOTAL ASSETS	**100.0 %**	**100.0 %**	**100.0 %**	**100.0 %**

Current liabilities	%	%	%	%
Long-term liabilities	%	%	%	%
Contributed capital	%	%	%	%
Retained earnings	%	%	%	%
Treasury stock and other stockholders' equity	%	%	%	%
TOTAL L & SE	**100.0 %**	**100.0 %**	**100.0 %**	**100.0 %**

Company Name: _____

CONDENSED
MULTI-STEP INCOME STATEMENT

Fiscal year ended... ($ in millions)	(Most recent year)			
Revenue	$	$	$	$
Cost of goods sold				
Gross profit				
Operating expenses				
Income from operations				
Other revenues and expenses				
Income from continuing operations before income tax				
Provision for income tax				
Income from continuing operations				
Nonrecurring items				
NET INCOME	$	$	$	$

Earnings per share				

Company Name: _____

CONDENSED MULTI-STEP INCOME STATEMENT
Trend Analysis

Fiscal year ended… ($ in millions)	_____ (Most recent year)	_____	_____	_____
Revenue				100
Cost of goods sold				100
Gross profit				**100**
Operating expenses				100
Income from operations				**100**
Other revenues and expenses				100
Income from continuing operations before income tax				**100**
Provision for income tax				100
Income from continuing operations				**100**
Nonrecurring items				100
NET INCOME				**100**

Earnings per share				100

Company Name: _____

CONDENSED MULTI-STEP INCOME STATEMENT
Common-Size Statements

Fiscal year ended... ($ in millions)	(Most recent year)			
Revenue	100.0 %	100.0 %	100.0 %	100.0 %
Cost of goods sold	%	%	%	%
Gross profit	%	%	%	%
Operating expenses	%	%	%	%
Income from operations	%	%	%	%
Other revenues and expenses	%	%	%	%
Income from continuing operations before income tax	%	%	%	%
Provision for income tax	%	%	%	%
Income from continuing operations	%	%	%	%
Nonrecurring items	%	%	%	%
NET INCOME	%	%	%	%

Company Name: _____

CONDENSED STATEMENT OF CASH FLOWS

Fiscal year ended... ($ in millions)	_____ (most recent year)	_____	_____	_____
Net cash from **operating activities**	$	$	$	$
Net cash from **investing activities**				
Net cash from **financing activities**				
Effect of **exchange rate** on cash				
Net change in cash				
Cash, beginning				
Cash, ending	$	$	$	$

CONDENSED STATEMENT OF CASH FLOWS
Trend Analysis

Fiscal year ended... ($ in millions)	_____ (most recent year)	_____	_____	_____
Net cash from **operating activities**				100
Net cash from **investing activities**				100
Net cash from **financing activities**				100
Effect of **exchange rate** on cash				100
Net change in cash				100
Cash, beginning				100
Cash, ending				100

Company Name: _____

STATEMENT OF CASH FLOWS

SOURCES AND USES OF CASH STATEMENT				
Fiscal year ended...				
Net cash from operating activities	$	$	$	$
Sale of property, plant, equipment				
Sale of investments				
Other investing cash flow items				
Issuance of debt				
Issuance of capital stock				
Other financing cash flow items				
Effect of exchange rate changes				
TOTAL Sources of cash	$	$	$	$
Purchase of property, plant, and equipment				
Purchase of investments				
Other investing cash flow items				
Repayment of debt				
Repurchase of capital stock				
Cash dividends paid				
Other financing cash flow items				
Effect of exchange rate changes				
TOTAL Uses of cash	$	$	$	$
Net change in cash	$	$	$	$

SOURCES AND USES OF CASH STATEMENT -- COMMON-SIZE STATEMENTS				
Fiscal year ended...				
Net cash from operating activities	%	%	%	%
Sale of property, plant, equipment	%	%	%	%
Sale of investments	%	%	%	%
Other investing cash flow items	%	%	%	%
Issuance of debt	%	%	%	%
Issuance of capital stock	%	%	%	%
Other financing cash flow items	%	%	%	%
Effect of exchange rate changes	%	%	%	%
TOTAL Sources of cash	**100%**	**100%**	**100%**	**100%**
Purchase of property, plant, and equipment	%	%	%	%
Purchase of investments	%	%	%	%
Other investing cash flow items	%	%	%	%
Repayment of debt	%	%	%	%
Repurchase of capital stock	%	%	%	%
Cash dividends paid	%	%	%	%
Other financing cash flow items	%	%	%	%
Effect of exchange rate changes	%	%	%	%
TOTAL Uses of cash	%	%	%	%
Net change in cash	%	%	%	%

Company Name: _____

Company Industry: _____

RATIO ANALYSIS WORKSHEET

Industry Norm		Fiscal year ended...		
SIC	RATIOS	————	————	————
	LIQUIDITY			
NA	Working capital	$	$	$
	Current ratio			
	Quick ratio			
	Cash flow liquidity ratio			
	LONG-TERM SOLVENCY			
	Debt ratio			
	Debt-to-equity ratio			
	Times-interest-earned			
NA	Free cash flow	$	$	$
	Cash flow adequacy			
	MANAGEMENT EFFICIENCY			
	Accounts receivable turnover			
	Inventory turnover			
	Asset turnover			
	Accounts payable turnover			
	Accounts receivable days			
	Inventory days			
	Accounts payable days			
	Net trade cycle			
	PROFITABILITY			
%	Gross profit margin	%	%	%
%	Return-on-sales (ROS)	%	%	%
%	Return-on-assets (ROA)	%	%	%
%	Return-on-equity (ROE)	%	%	%
$	Earnings per share	$	$	$
	Quality of income			
	INVESTMENT			
	Price/Earnings ratio (PE)			
%	Dividend yield	%	%	%
$	Dividend rate	$	$	$
$	Book value per share	$	$	$
	Market value per share:			
NA	Close (Date) _____	$	$	$
NA	52-week high	$	$	$
NA	52-week low	$	$	$

APPENDIX A – FEATURED CORPORATIONS

For each corporation used in the text, following is a description of the company, its stock symbol, and the corporate website.

Allied Waste Industries, Inc. (AW NYSE) is the #2 waste-hauler (Waste Management, Inc. is #1) that does business in every major facet of the nonhazardous solid waste industry. It serves 10 million customers through its network of collection companies, transfer stations, active landfills, and recycling facilities. The company has reorganized and is expanding through internal growth and vertical integration.   www.alliedwaste.com

Amazon.com, Inc. (AMZN NASDAQ) is the world's largest bookstore offering millions of books, CDs, DVDs, videos, and other products at its Web site. After years of expansion, the company is now focusing on profits. Founder Jeff Bezos and his family own about one-third of the company.   www.amazon.com

American Eagle Outfitters, Inc. (AEOS NASDAQ) is a retailer that designs, markets and sells its own brand of clothing targeting 15 to 25-year-olds in the United States and Canada. American Eagle operates over 800 stores in the United States and Canada and also distributes merchandise via its e-commerce operation.   www.ae.com

Anheuser-Busch Companies, Inc. (BUD NYSE) is the world's largest brewer and the largest beer producer in the United States with approximately half of the market share. It makes Budweiser, the nation's top-ranked beer, along with Bud Light, Michelob, and Busch. It is the largest recycler of aluminum cans in the world and one of the largest manufacturers of aluminum cans in the United States. Approximately 94% of the Company's net sales are generated in the United States. It also operates amusement parks Busch Gardens and Sea World.   www.anheuser-busch.com

Apple Computer, Inc. (AAPL NASDAQ) designs, manufactures, and markets personal computers primarily for education, creative, consumer, and business customers. The company now also offers digital music players (iPod) and an online music store (iTunes). Other products include servers (Xserve), wireless networking equipment (Airport), and publishing and multimedia software.   www.apple.com

Applebee's International, Inc. (APPB NASDAQ) operates over 800 casual dining restaurants under the name Applebee's Neighborhood Grill & Bar.   www.applebees.com

Borders Group (BGP NYSE) operates book, music, and movie superstores, as well as mall-based bookstores. Its stores offer an assortment of books, and music and movies; new releases, hardcover and paperback bestsellers, periodicals, and a selection of other titles; and gifts and stationery merchandise, as well as feature cafes and browsing center. The company operates over 500 superstores under the Borders name in the United States, United Kingdom, Australia, Puerto Rico, New Zealand, and Singapore, as well as over 600 mall-based bookstores primarily under the Waldenbooks name in the United States and Books etc. in the United Kingdom. Borders Group owns and operates the United Kingdom-based Paperchase Products Limited and was founded in 1971.   www.bordersgroupinc.com

Carnival Corporation (CCL NYSE) (used to be Carnival Cruise Lines Inc.) provides cruises to major vacation destinations outside the Far East. It also markets and operates hotels or lodges, motor coaches for sightseeing and charters, domed rail cars, and luxury day boats. The company operates over 75 cruise ships with about 130,000 passenger capacity in North America, Europe, the United Kingdom, Germany, Australia, and New Zealand.   www.carnivalcorp.com

Circuit City Stores (CC NYSE) operates as a specialty retailer of consumer electronics, home office products, entertainment software, and related services. The Domestic segment operates over 600 superstores and the International segment offers private-label and brand-name consumer electronics products in Canada.   www.circuitcity.com

Coca-Cola Company, The (KO NYSE) was established in 1886 and is now the world's largest soft drink company operating in approximately 200 countries and commanding approximately 50% of the global soft-drink market. The firm, which does no bottling, sells about 300 drink brands, including Coca-Cola, Sprite, Barq's, Minute Maid, and Dasani and Evian water. www.cocacola.com

Darden Restaurants, Inc. (DRI NYSE) is a dining restaurant company that operates over 1,300 restaurants in the United States and Canada, including Red Lobster, Olive Garden, Bahama Breeze, Smokey Bones Barbeque & Grill, and Three Seasons.   www.darden.com

Dell (DELL NASDAQ) is the world's #1 direct-sale computer vendor and is competing with Hewlett-Packard for the worldwide PC title. In addition to a full line of desktop and notebook computers designed for consumers, Dell offers network servers, workstations, storage systems, and Ethernet switches for enterprise customers. Dell's growing services unit provides systems integration, support, and training.   www.dell.com

Ford Motor Company (F NYSE) began a manufacturing revolution in the 1900s with its mass production assembly lines. Now the company is the world's largest pickup truck maker and the #2 producer of vehicles behind General Motors. Vehicles are produced under the names of Ford, Jaguar, Lincoln, Mercury, Volvo, and Aston Martin. Ford has a controlling interest in Mazda and has purchased BMW's Land Rover SUV operations. It also owns the #1 auto finance company, Ford Motor Credit, and Hertz, the world's #1 car-rental firm. The Ford family owns about 40% of the company's voting stock.   www.ford.com

Gap Inc., The (GPS NYSE) operates over 4,200 clothing stores including casual styles at The Gap, GapKids, and BabyGap, fast-growing budget Old Navy, and the chic Banana Republic. All Gap clothing is private-label merchandise made specifically for the company. From the design board to store displays, the company controls all aspects of its trademark casual look. The founding Fisher family owns about a third of the company.   www.gap.com

Gateway Inc. (GTW NYSE) sells desktop and notebook computers, servers, and PC-related products and services. Gateway offers its PCs under two brand names, Gateway and eMachines. www.gateway.com

General Electric Company (GE NYSE) is one of the top players in a vast array of markets including: aircraft engines, locomotives and other transportation equipment, appliances (kitchen and laundry equipment), lighting, electric distribution and control equipment, generators and turbines, nuclear reactors, medical imaging equipment, and plastics. Its financial arm accounts for nearly half of the company's revenues, making GE one of the largest financial services companies in the U.S. Other operations include the NBC television network.   www.ge.com

General Motors Corporation (GM NYSE) is the world's #1 maker of cars and trucks, with brands such as Buick, Cadillac, Chevrolet, GMC, Pontiac, Saab, and Saturn. It also designs and manufactures locomotives (GM Locomotive) and heavy-duty transmissions (Allison Transmission). Other nonautomotive operations include DirecTV (Hughes Electronics) and subsidiary GMAC provides financing. www.gm.com

Google Inc. (GOOG NASDAQ) maintains an index of Websites and its search technology enables people to obtain nearly instant access to relevant information online. Google offers its services and products free of charge and generates revenue primarily by delivering online advertising. www.google.com

Harley-Davidson Inc. (HDI NYSE) produces heavyweight motorcycles, motorcycle parts, and related accessories. It operates in two segments, Motorcycles and Related Products and Financial Services. The Motorcycles and Related Products segment engages in the design, manufacture, and sale of primarily heavyweight, touring, custom, and performance motorcycles, as well as a line of motorcycle parts, accessories, clothing, and collectibles. www.harley-davidson.com

Hewlett-Packard Company (HPQ NYSE) is a provider of computing and imaging solutions for business and home. The company provides enterprise and consumer customers a full range of high-tech products, including personal computers, servers, storage products, printers, software, and computer-related services. CEO Carly Fiorina lead the largest deal in tech sector history -- the acquisition of Compaq Computer -- in a stock transaction valued at approximately $19 billion. www.hp.com

International Business Machines (IBM NYSE) is an information technology (IT) company. IBM also provides business, technology and consulting services. The majority of the Company's enterprise business, which excludes the company's original equipment manufacturer (OEM) technology business, occurs in industries that are broadly grouped into six sectors: financial services, public, industrial, distribution, communications and small and medium business. www.ibm.com

Intel Corporation (INTC NASDAQ) is the largest producer of semiconductors in the world currently possessing 80% of the market share. Intel's most notable products include its Pentium and Celeron microprocessors. Intel also makes flash memories and is #1 globally in this market. Dell is the company's largest customer. www.intel.com

J.C. Penney Company Inc. (JCP NYSE) provides merchandise and services to consumers through its department stores and Direct (catalog/Internet). The Company markets family apparel, jewelry, shoes, accessories, and home furnishings. In addition, the department stores provide customers with additional services such as salon, optical, portrait photography, and custom decorating. Their brands include The Original Arizona Jean Company; Worthington; Stafford; nicole by Nicole Miller; Bisou Bisou by Michele Bohbot; Solitude by Shaun Tomson, and Chris Madden for JCPenney Home Collection. www.jcpenney.com

Landry's Restaurants, Inc. (LNY NYSE) has an array of formats, menus, and price points that appeal to a range of markets and customer tastes. The Company is also engaged in the ownership and operation of select hospitality businesses, including hotel and casino resorts that provide dining, leisure and entertainment experiences. In 2005, Golden Nugget Hotels and Casinos in downtown Las Vegas and Laughlin, Nevada were acquired. www.landrysrestaurants.com

McDonald's Corporation (MCD NYSE) is the world's #1 fast-food chain, operating more than 30,000 restaurants in 121 countries worldwide. In addition to the familiar freestanding locations, McDonald's has mini-restaurants at locations within Wal-Mart and Chevron stores. In addition to the burger business, McDonald's owns the Donatos Pizza chain and the 650-unit Boston Market chain. Much of the new growth is in foreign markets that now generate over 60% of sales. www.mcdonalds.com

Microsoft Corporation (MSFT NASDAQ) is the world's #1 software company that develops, manufactures, licenses, and supports a variety of products and services, including its Windows operating systems and Office software suite. The company has expanded into markets such as video game consoles, interactive television, and Internet access. It is also targeting services for growth, looking to transform its software applications into Web-based services for enterprises and consumers. The Company sells the Xbox video game console, along with games and peripherals. Microsoft has reached a tentative settlement to end an ongoing antitrust investigation, agreeing to uniformly license its operating systems and allow manufacturers to include competing software with Windows. www.microsoft.com

Oracle Corporation (ORCL NASDAQ) is a leading provider of systems software, offering a variety of business applications that include software for data warehousing, customer relationship management, and supply chain management. Oracle's software runs on a broad range of computers including mainframes, workstations, desktops, laptops, and handheld devices. Oracle also provides consulting, support, and training services. www.oracle.com

PepsiCo, Inc. (PEP NYSE) is the world's #2 soft-drink maker and the world's #1 maker of snacks. Beverages include Pepsi (the #2 soft drink), Mountain Dew, Slice, Tropicana Juices (the world's leading juice manufacturer), Aquafina bottled water, All-Sport, Dole juices, and Lipton tea. PepsiCo also owns Frito-Lay, the world's #1 maker of snacks such as corn chips (Doritos, Fritos) and potato chips (Lay's, Ruffles, WOW!). Its international divisions operate in over 200 countries, with its largest operations in Mexico and the United Kingdom. www.pepsico.com

Royal Caribbean Cruises Ltd. (RCL NYSE) is the world's second-largest cruise line (behind Carnival) providing cruises to Alaska, the Caribbean, and Europe on 25 different cruise ships. The firm's two cruise brands, Celebrity Cruises and Royal Caribbean International, carry over two million passengers a year to about 200 destinations. www.rccl.com

Southwest Airlines Co. (LUV NYSE) has expanded its low-cost, no-frills approach to air travel throughout the US to service over 60 cities in 30 states. Its approach to cutting costs includes ticketless travel on only Boeing 737s, which resulted in 30 straight profitable years. www.southwest.com

Starbucks Corporation (SBUX NASDAQ) is the leading specialty coffee retailer with 5,900 coffee shops positioned throughout 25 countries in office buildings, malls, airports, and other locations. In addition to coffee, Starbucks offers coffee beans, pastries, mugs, coffee makers, coffee grinders, and even coffee ice cream. The company also sells its beans to restaurants, businesses, airlines, and hotels, and offers mail order and online catalogs. Starbucks has expanded into Frappuccino, a bottled coffee drink, jointly with PepsiCo. www.starbucks.com

Trump Organization, The is privately owned by Donald Trump and controls several New York real estate pieces including Trump International Hotel, Trump Tower (26 floors), 40 Wall Street, and 50% of the General Motors Building. Trump also has a 42% stake in Trump Hotels & Casino Resorts, which operate three casinos in Atlantic City, and 50% of the Miss USA, Miss Teen USA, and Miss Universe beauty pageants. (212) 832-2000

United Airlines Corporation (UAUA NASDAQ) transports persons, property, and mail throughout the United States and abroad. United is a passenger airline with more than 3,600 flights a day to more than 200 destinations through its mainline and United Express services in 28 countries and two United States territories. In February 2006, the Company emerged out of bankruptcy. www.united.com

Wal-Mart Stores, Inc. (WMT NYSE) is the largest retailer in the world with over 4,600 stores. Its sales are greater than Sears, Target, and Kroger combined. Its stores include Wal-Mart discount stores, Wal-Mart Supercenters that are a combination discount and grocery store, and Sam's Club membership-only warehouse stores. Most Wal-Mart stores are in the United States, but international expansion has made it the #1 retailer in Canada and Mexico. Wal-Mart also has operations in South America, Asia, and Europe. www.walmartstores.com

Yum! Brands, Inc. (YUM NYSE) is the largest restaurant operator in terms of locations (second to McDonald's in sales) with over 34,000 units in more than 100 countries. YUM consists of six operating segments: KFC, Pizza Hut, Taco Bell, Long John Silver's (LJS), and A&W All-American Food Restaurants (A&W), YUM Restaurants International, and YUM Restaurants China. www.yum.com

APPENDIX B – RATIOS

Ratios are extremely valuable as analytical tools, but they also have limitations. They can indicate areas of strength and weakness, but do not provide answers. To be most effective, they should be used in combination with other elements of financial analysis. Also, please note that there is not one definitive set of key financial ratios, no uniform definition for all ratios, and no standard which should be met for each ratio. Each situation should be evaluated within the context of the particular firm, industry, and economic environment.

There are five major categories of ratios listed to help analyze a particular aspect of the financial condition. Categories and ratios are described on the following pages.

LIQUIDITY	LONG-TERM SOLVENCY	MANAGEMENT EFFICIENCY	PROFITABILITY	INVESTMENT
Working Capital	Debt Ratio	Accounts Receivable Turnover	Gross Profit Margin (GP%)	Price/Earnings (P/E)
Current Ratio	Debt-to-Equity Ratio	Inventory Turnover	Return On Sales (ROS)	Dividend Yield
Quick Ratio	Times-Interest-Earned	Asset Turnover	Return On Assets (ROA)	Dividend Rate
Cash Flow Liquidity Ratio	Free Cash Flow	Accounts Payable Turnover	Return On Equity (ROE)	Book Value Per Share
	Cash Flow Adequacy	Accounts Receivable Days	DuPont Analysis Of Roe	
		Inventory Days	Financial Leverage Percentage	
		Accounts Payable Days	Earnings Per Share (EPS)	
		Net Trade Cycle	Quality of Income	

RATIO CATEGORIES

LIQUIDITY measures a firm's ability to meet cash needs as they arise.

LONG-TERM SOLVENCY measures the extent of debt relative to equity, if financial leverage is being used effectively, and the ability to cover interest, investing activity, financing activity, and other fixed payment requirements.

MANAGEMENT EFFICIENCY measures the efficiency of managing cash, accounts receivable, inventory, property, plant, and equipment, and accounts payable.

PROFITABILITY measures the ability to generate profits; the overall performance of a firm.

INVESTMENT compares the market value per share to other per share amounts and indicates the level of dividend payment.

LIQUIDITY

WORKING CAPITAL	Current assets - Current liabilities
Working capital is the amount by which current assets exceed current liabilities. It measures the cushion of funds maintained to allow for the uneven flow of working capital.	

CURRENT RATIO	Current assets / Current liabilities
The **current ratio** measures the ability to pay current payables as they come due. It compares current assets to current liabilities because current assets are generally used to meet current liability obligations. It presents working capital information in a ratio format.	

QUICK RATIO	(Cash + Short-term investments + Accounts receivable) / Current liabilities
The **quick ratio** compares assets that can be quickly liquidated to current liabilities. It is a more rigorous measure of short-term liquidity than the current ratio. This ratio is also referred to as the *acid-test ratio*.	

CASH FLOW LIQUIDITY RATIO	(Cash + Marketable securities + NCOA) / Current liabilities
The **cash-flow-liquidity ratio** compares cash resources to current liabilities. This ratio uses cash and marketable securities (truly liquid current assets) and net cash from operating activities to evaluate whether adequate cash is generated from selling inventory and offering services. Even a profitable business will fail without sufficient cash. It is a cash-basis measure of short-term liquidity.	

LONG-TERM SOLVENCY

DEBT RATIO	Total liabilities / Total assets
The **debt ratio** measures the proportion of all assets financed by debt by comparing total liabilities to total assets. A higher ratio indicates greater financial risk.	

DEBT-TO-EQUITY RATIO	Total liabilities / Total stockholders' equity
The **debt-to-equity ratio** measures the risk of a firm's capital structure by comparing the funds provided by creditors (debt) with those provided by shareholders (equity). It helps analysts evaluate the trade offs between risk and return. It offers the same information as the debt ratio, but presents it in a different format.	

TIMES-INTEREST-EARNED	Income from operations / Interest expense
The **times-interest-earned** ratio reflects the ability to pay interest expense by measuring the number of times operating income covers interest expense. The fixed interest payments that accompany debt must be satisfied from operating earnings. This ratio is also referred to as the *interest coverage ratio*.	

FREE CASH FLOW	Net cash from operating activities (NCOA) - Capital expenditures required to maintain productive capacity - Dividends paid
Free cash flow reflects the amount of cash available for business activities after allowances for investing and financing activity requirements to maintain productive capacity at current levels. Adequate free cash flow allows for growth and financial flexibility.	

CASH FLOW ADEQUACY	Net cash from operating activities (NCOA) / (Capital expenditures required to maintain productive capacity + Dividends paid)
The **cash-flow-adequacy** ratio evaluates whether cash flow from operating activities is sufficient to cover annual payment requirements. The above ratio is defined to evaluate whether cash flow from operating activities is adequate to maintain productive capacity at current levels. It presents free cash flow information in a ratio format. This ratio (with modifications in the denominator) is used by credit-rating agencies to identify if there is adequate cash coverage of capital expenditures, dividends, debt, and other annual payments.	

MANAGEMENT EFFICIENCY

ACCOUNTS RECEIVABLE TURNOVER	Revenue / Accounts receivable*
The **accounts receivable turnover (A/R T/O)** ratio indicates how many times average accounts receivable are collected annually. The longer receivables are outstanding, the higher the collection risk. Receivables must be managed efficiently since they are financed using some cost of capital and entail collection risk.	

INVENTORY TURNOVER	Cost of goods sold / Inventory*

The **inventory turnover (Inventory T/O)** ratio indicates the number of times a company sells its average inventory level during the year. Inventory is costly in terms of financing and storage, so companies want enough inventory to meet customer demand without stock-outs.

ACCOUNTS PAYABLE TURNOVER	Cost of goods sold / Accounts payable*

The **accounts payable turnover (A/P T/O)** ratio indicates the number of times a company pays its average accounts payable level during the year. This must be efficiently managed to make use of low-cost supplier financing and not to delay payment to the extent that would damage supplier relations.

ASSET TURNOVER	Revenue / Total assets*

The **asset turnover** ratio evaluates how efficiently assets are used to produce revenues by comparing revenue to total assets. This ratio is a measure of asset management efficiency and of profitability.

ACCOUNTS RECEIVABLE DAYS	360 days in the year / Accounts receivable turnover

Accounts receivable days indicate the average number of days required to convert receivables into cash. It offers the same information as the accounts receivable turnover ratio, but presents it in a different format.

INVENTORY DAYS	360 days in the year / Inventory turnover

Inventory days indicate the average length of time that inventories are available for sale. It offers the same information as the inventory turnover ratio, but presents it in a different format.

ACCOUNTS PAYABLE DAYS	360 days in the year / Accounts payable turnover

Accounts payable days indicate the average length of time that accounts payable remain outstanding. It offers the same information as the accounts payable turnover ratio, but presents it in a different format.

NET TRADE CYCLE	Accounts receivable days + Inventory days - Accounts payable days

The **net trade cycle** measures the number of days in the normal operating cycle that includes purchasing inventory on credit, selling the inventory and creating accounts receivable, and collecting the cash from customers. This breakdown of the cycle helps analysts understand why cash flow generation from operating activities has improved or deteriorated. The longer the net trade cycle, the larger the working capital requirement. Also referred to as the *cash conversion cycle*.

* Average amounts may be used to calculate the formula to better represent the balance in the account over the entire year.

PROFITABILITY

GROSS PROFIT MARGIN	Gross profit / Revenue

The **gross profit margin (GP%)** measures the ability of a firm to control the costs of inventory or production (COGS, the most significant operating expense for retail and manufacturing firms) by comparing operating revenue with gross profit. This ratio is the first measure of profitability.

RETURN ON SALES (ROS)	Net income / Revenue

The **return-on-sales** ratio measures the profitability of each dollar of revenue. It expresses net income as a % of revenue that represents the firm's ability to translate revenue into profits. It measures profitability after consideration of all revenues and expenses, including operating, non-operating, and special one-time items. This ratio is also referred to as *net profit margin*.

RETURN ON ASSETS (ROA)	ROA = Net income / Total assets* **
	ROA = ROS x ASSET TURNOVER
	ROA = (NI / Revenue) x (Revenue / Total assets)

The **return-on-assets** ratio measures how efficiently assets are used to produce profits (net income). A high ROA ratio depends on managing asset investments to produce the greatest amount of revenue and controlling expenses to keep net income high. ROA is the most comprehensive measure of profitability since it takes into account both the profitability of each dollar of revenue (ROS) and sales volume (Asset T/O). ROS x Asset T/O = ROA. Analyze the components, ROS and Asset Turnover, to better understand corporate strategy*** and why ROA has changed from prior years. ROA can be compared with alternative investments, segments within the company, and other companies to measure the effectiveness of planning and control.

RETURN ON EQUITY (ROE)	(Net income - Preferred dividends) / Common stockholders' equity*

The **return-on-equity** ratio measures how efficiently amounts invested by common shareholders are used to generate profits. Review the **DuPont Analysis of ROE** (following) to evaluate how the three components of ROE interrelate to produce the overall return to shareholders. If there is no preferred stock the ROE formula = Net income / SE.

DUPONT ANALYSIS OF ROE	ROE = Net income / SE*
	ROE = ROS x ASSET T/O x FINANCIAL LEVERAGE
	ROE = (NI / Revenue) x (Revenue / Total assets*) x (Total assets* / SE*)

The components of **ROE** help to better assess company performance and indicate ways that management can improve ROE. The first two components comprise ROA (ROS x ASSET TURNOVER). Therefore, improving ROA also results in increasing ROE. The third component, FINANCIAL LEVERAGE, is the effective use of debt in a capital structure. It increases when ROA is higher than the cost of debt, because the excess return accrues to the benefit of the shareholders. To summarize, ROE = ROA x FINANCIAL LEVERAGE or ROE / ROA = FINANCIAL LEVERAGE.

FINANCIAL LEVERAGE PERCENTAGE	ROE - ROA

The **financial leverage percentage** is the portion of ROE that results from the use of financial leverage. Leverage is positive when a company borrows at one rate and invests at a higher rate of return. Stated another way, ROE = ROA (the return from operations) + Financial Leverage Percentage (the return from use of financial leverage.)

EARNINGS PER SHARE (EPS)	(Net income - Preferred dividends) / Number of common shares outstanding

Earnings per share indicate the amount of net income earned for one share of the company's common stock outstanding. It is probably the single most watched ratio. Compare EPS to other per share amounts such as the market price per share (Price/Earnings ratio) and dividends per share (Dividend Payout ratio) to reveal additional information.

QUALITY OF INCOME	Net cash from operating activities (NCOA) / Net income

The **quality-of-income** ratio compares cash flows from operating activities to net income. A ratio higher than 1.0 indicates high-quality income because each dollar of net income is supported by one dollar or more of cash. It is cash (not accrual-based net income) that is needed to pay suppliers and employees, to invest in income-producing assets, and to ensure long-term success.

* Average amounts may be used to calculate the formula to better represent the balance in the account over the entire year.

** Alternate formula for ROA = [Net income before nonrecurring items + Interest expense (net of tax)] / Average total assets. This is a more complex formula that incorporates interest expense as the return on liabilities to creditors and net income as the return to shareholders. A = L + SE.

***Essentially, there are two business strategies: (1) The high-value or product-differentiation strategy relies on the superiority or distinctiveness of the products. This allows charging higher prices and then earning greater ROS. (2) The low-cost strategy relies on efficient management of assets to produce high asset turnover ratios.

INVESTMENT

PRICE/EARNINGS (P/E)	Market price per share of common stock / Earnings per share

The **price/earnings ratio** indicates the market price of one dollar of earnings. It expresses the relationship between a company's earnings per share and the market price per common share. It is a measure of shareholder perception and helps to evaluate a potential investment.

DIVIDEND YIELD	Dividends per share of common stock / Market price per share of common stock

The **dividend yield** indicates the portion of a stock's market value returned to the shareholder in the form of a dividend. It is a measure of dividends paid and helps evaluate a potential investment.

DIVIDEND RATE	Cash dividends per share

The **dividend rate** indicates the amount of dividends per share paid out over the past 12 months.

BOOK VALUE PER SHARE	(Total stockholders' equity - Preferred equity) / Number of shares of common stock outstanding

The **book value per share** of common stock indicates the recorded accounting amount of common stockholders' equity per share of common stock outstanding. It can help to evaluate a potential investment when compared to the market value per share.